The Spiritual Journey of A Legend: The Life of Reverend Dr. James W. Sanders

as told to

Toschia

The Spiritual Journey of A Legend:
The Life of Reverend Dr. James W. Sanders

as told to
Toschia

Divine Literary Publications

San Antonio, Texas

DIVINE LITERARY PUBLICATIONS

San Antonio, Texas

Copyright February 2015, Divine Literary Publications

ISBN 978-0-9709957-8-0

Printed in the United States of America

Inside text design: Mark Mayfield

Printed in the United States of America

DEDICATION

First and most important, I dedicate my life story to my Lord and Savior Jesus Christ and to my precious wife for fifty-eight years, Rubye Sanders. I also wish to dedicate this work to my three wonderful children, Jewette, James Jr., and Ruzlin, also to my grandchildren, great grandchildren, to the church in which I was pastor for sixty-one years, Bethel Baptist in Gaffney, to Island Creek Baptist Church, Seek Well Baptist Church and of course my home church, Corinth in Union. And finally to my very dear and close friend Reverend Malachi Duncan, to all the preachers and pastors of the Gospel and the countless people I visited in hospitals, prisons, nursing homes and everywhere else the Lord called me to administer His word to the lost and needy.

ACKNOWLEDGMENTS

The family of Reverend Dr. James W. Sanders Sr., would first and most important acknowledge God and our savior Jesus Christ for what they have done in our life and for the salvation brought to our house, our race, our country and the world. We acknowledge all the men and women who helped make this re-creation of Reverend Sanders's life a reality. We thank Reverend Malachi Duncan, Reverend Latta Thomas, Reverend A.L. Brackett, and Reverend C.V. Owens and Reverend Matthew Zimmerman. We also thank Mandrick Wilkins, Jack Millwood, Mayor Henry Jolly, Barry Wynn, Agnes Bright, Martha Montgomery, Charles Montgomery, Congressman John Spratt and Congressman James Clyburn for their assistance. And the family extends their extreme gratitude to Toschia for capturing the story, to Professor Frederick Williams for writing the story and Divine Literary Publications for publishing and therefore, assuring the legacy of Reverend Sanders will live on in the history of ministry in South Carolina. Finally, a special thank you to Marionette Daniels, Reverend Sanders's older sister, who is the only person that knew Reverend Sanders from birth to his passing in 2010. We would like to acknowledge and thank the entire Bethel Baptist family for the 61 years they loved and worshipped with Reverend Sanders.

FOREWORD

Let me begin by saying that I am currently writing my own memoirs. I know the challenge of encapsulating one's life into words on a page. Professor Frederick Williams and AttorneyToschia Moffett, the two writers of this positive portrayal of a great man, have done a remarkable job in not only telling the story of Reverend James W. Sanders, Sr.'s life, but they brought this incredible leader to life for future generations. I know firsthand the tremendous force that he was, and through this great work, he can continue to teach and lead others as he did when he was among us.

Reverend Sanders was a dear friend and mentor to me and many others. He had the uncanny ability to frame an argument in such a way that you could not find fault with his logic. He was a calm, solid rock in the face of much tumult and angst. He was truly grounded and guided throughout his life by his faith in the Creator and his belief that his steps were ordered.

As the son of a minister, I knew the expectation that sons, especially those of us who are the first born, should follow their fathers into the ministry. Growing up, I felt this was the path that awaited me as well. Yet, when I attended South Carolina State College, now University, and took on a leadership role in the civil rights protests that emanated from that campus in 1960, my life was forever changed. It was through the teachings of my fundamentalist father, who told me "son, the world would rather see a sermon than hear one," and through the support of other clergy like Reverend Sanders that I found my calling in public service. While great men like Enos Clyburn and James Sanders used the pulpit to bring about change, I decided that the way best suited for me to challenge the injustice and irreverence in our government was to work from within that system. And I feel that my steps were ordered as well.

While our paths were divergent, our motivations and our strengths were very much the same. We both lived by the admonition in *First Peter 4:10*, "As each has received a gift, use it to serve one another as good stewards of God's varied grace."

Reverend Sanders was a true steward of the gifts that had been given to him. As the writers show so eloquently in *The Spiritual Journey of a Legend,* even the most humble of men can grow into leaders. Reverend Sanders' journey began in the country town of Union, South Carolina, and his path didn't lead him far afield--just to the next county and another small town called Gaffney. While the miles of his life's journey were short, the impact of that life was far and wide.

Reverend Sanders deeply felt the sting of injustice and was dedicated to ending injustice in any form. This book tells the story of one of the many unsung heroes to emerge from the segregated South. Reverend Sanders' journey is like so many who dedicated their lives to making their communities better for future generations. There is no question that he knew the work that he did was ordained. It was not his choice, but his calling and he never wavered. This is a story of hope, of courage, of determination and of absolute faith.

He and I both share a life's journey that was guided by the principle laid out in *Matthew 25:45*, "As you did it to one of the least of these my brothers, you did it to me."

Reverend Sanders' favorite gospel was *Traveling Shoes* and the lyrics say, *"Got my traveling shoes and I can travel now."* This extraordinary work of creative non-fiction has become those traveling shoes, and will enable Reverend Sanders' story to travel now so this important voice will not be silenced.

Congressman James Clyburn

PROLOGUE

The drive down to Spartanburg, South Carolina from Columbia will take about an hour; just enough time for me to relax and reflect on the past twelve hours..The warm rays from the sun shining through the window of my cousins Chrysler 300 feels good against my skin. It is stimulating and I know I will need every bit of help because of the enormous task I am about to take on for the next six months. All my life I welcomed challenges and when I received the call from Reverend James William Sanders Sr., last night I knew I was about to encounter another major challenge and this one of enormous importance.

I sit in the den of my home in Killeen, Texas watching the Rachel Maddow show when the phone rang a little after eight o'clock in the evening. My first inclination is not to answer it because Rachel was in the middle of a hot debate with some member of the Tea Party. I didn't want to be distracted or miss any of the hot exchange between the two. But I check the I.D. and see who is calling; I hit the "Pause" button on the remote and pick up the telephone.

"Dr. Sanders, how are you sir?" I ask.

"I'm doing as God would have me," he says.

"To what do I owe the privilege of this call?"

There is a slight pause and he seems to be breathing quite heavily. I wait for his response.

"Can you be here by tomorrow afternoon?" he asks.

Now it is my turn to pause. By tomorrow afternoon, what is the rush? He sounds a little strange in his tone, almost a hint of desperation.

"Dr. Sanders, it's after nine o'clock here in Texas, and I'd have to pack and get my dogs taken care of. I don't know if I can do all that, then get a flight and be there by noon." I listen to his breathing increase. "Where are you?"

"In the hospital right now," he says. "I'll probably be here for a while."

"Are you sick…" I stop but it is too late. Obviously he is sick. He is calling from the hospital. I know he has been ill. He had gotten sick a couple of weeks ago when I was in Gaffney, South Carolina assisting him to plan a cultural event at his church.

"Nothing real serious, but yes I am."

For some reason I don't feel that he is being honest with me. I have to probe a little deeper.

"What is it?" I ask. "Is it a relapse from your operation last year?"

"I guess I'm just getting old," he chuckles. "They'll be taking a series of tests tomorrow morning and be finished by the time you get here in the afternoon."

"Dr. Sanders, I'm not sure—"

"James Jr., will get your ticket tonight and you can pick it up at the airport," he cuts me off. "Don't you have an airport there or should he book you out of Dallas or Austin?"

"Dr. Sanders I don't know if—"

I am cut off. "Young lady I need you here because quite honestly I don't know how much more time God is going to give me to do His work here. I'm getting a very strong feeling that He wants me back home. I know He's got a special assignment waiting for me." He pauses.

I wait for him to continue. He is in charge and I know that is how it should be. I have immense respect for this man who has, over the years, accomplished so much.

"But it is important that I finish my work here and that's where you become important." Again, a slight pause and more heavy breathing. "We must write our own history for future generations," he continues. "Do you know who Reverend Richard Allen was?" He asks.

"Yes, he was the minister who broke with the Methodists in the early Nineteenth Century and established the separate Black Methodist church."

"Very good. Now do you know who Andrew Bryan was?'

"No."

"He gathered a small group of Blacks in Savannah, Georgia in the 1780s and held prayer meetings. He and his brother Sampson were arrested and whipped a number of times by the white authorities that didn't want them holding service unless sanctioned by the whites."

"I didn't know that."

"So if a real smart and educated lady like you didn't know that, just think how much less our people not educated like you know." He coughs and momentarily stops. "Young lady do you know who Christopher Rush, Theodore Wright, and Henry Highland Garnet were?"

"No sir, I have to say I don't recognize any of those names." I was beginning to feel rather uninformed about men whom, I assumed, were important historical figures in the church at one time.

"Church history is the foundation of our culture here in America. No wonder so many of our young don't attend church today. They don't know how important the church was to our ancestors. It was because of their unwavering faith in God and Jesus that they made it through."

"I understand and agree, but about tomorrow Dr. Sanders—,"

"These were Christian men who were always there when their beleaguered and sometimes beaten people came to them for consolation and most often, answers."

"I understand Dr. Sanders, but what does that have to do with me coming to Gaffney in the morning?"

"We must also record our history right here in Gaffney, South Carolina during some of the most turbulent years. I've been a minister for sixty-one years and like Reverend Allen, Dr. Benjamin Mays, Reverend Abernathy and King, I've experienced a lot of joy, pain, heartbreak, and special times with my people and I want to share all of that with the world."

"And rightfully so," I say.

"You, young lady and your publishing company are going to make this happen. I want you to write my story and that's why I need you here by tomorrow afternoon."

I practically drop the phone.

"You still there?" he asks.

"Yes sir, I am," I answer. "But may I ask why me?"

"Because I believe in you. Now I'm going to call James Jr., and have him make your reservation. Good night and I'll see you sometime tomorrow afternoon." Dr. Sanders finishes and hangs up.

His final words resonate with me the entire night, during my flight and now as I make my way off Highway 85 and head to the hospital.

"Because I believe in you," was one of the best compliments I'd ever received. I was about to capture the life of a Black man whose achievements are on the same plane as other famous South Carolinians like Robert Smalls, Joseph Rainey, and Dr. Benjamin Mays and he has enough confidence in me to successfully record his life for posterity.

I pull into the hospital parking lot, find a visitor space and park the Ford. I take in a deep breath and slowly release it. I am about to embark on a trip back into history and for that reason I smile, get out of the car and hurry inside. That morning Mrs. Sanders had placed my name on the visitors list since Reverend Sanders is in the Intensive Care Unit. I approach the desk and give the nurse my name. Just as I finish, Mrs. Sanders strolls out of the room right in front of me. I rush over to her.

"How is he?" I ask.

"He's strong and his will power is to hang on until the Lord wants him," she says. "He's been waiting for you. He has a fabulous story to tell about perseverance and trust in the Lord. God will let him tell you the story so you can write for the entire world to read." She finishes, pats me on my shoulder and walks down the corridor toward the exit.

As I stroll into Dr. Sanders' room I notice a glow all over his face. It conveys a message that this is a man quite content within himself. He has needles in both arms as he is being fed intravenously, and there is a tube in his mouth making it difficult for him to talk, but he manages. He scoots his body up and rests against the backboard of the bed. He motions for me to sit in the chair on the side of the bed.

"Thank you for coming," he says.

"It was kind of rough on such short notice but I made it."

"I'm sorry but I had no choice. God has given me a short notice on my time left for me on this side."

"How do you feel?" I ask.

"Pretty good," he says. "Where do you want to start?" he asks, evidently anxious to get started.

I pull my recorder out of my bag, relax back in the chair and hit the record button. "From the beginning, Dr. Sanders."

1.

Mama gave birth to me at home in her bedroom. We were awfully poor as were most Black people living in the rural town of Union, South Carolina in 1929. The thought of Mama delivering at a hospital was out of the question. She didn't even have a doctor to assist in bringing me into this world; instead my great aunt delivered me. During that time Mama and Poppa lived in a home right next to my paternal grandparents. It was a small two-bedroom house with a very small living room and kitchen. There was no running water inside the house and we had to go outside to use the outhouse. We bathed in a round silver galvanized tub located in the back yard.

It was a common practice for young couples to live very close to one of their parents. In our case it was Grandpa and Grandma Sanders because they were the more stable of the two families. Mama came from a relatively large family. She had seven brothers and sisters and right after they moved from the country up to Union, her father left the family and moved to Chicago. No one ever told us why Grandpa Willie left, but probably had something to do with the frustration Black men had to endure, not only in South Carolina but throughout the South during the early decades of the Twentieth Century. There was no "roaring Twenties" in South Carolina, especially for Black men. With eight children and no husband, Grandma did survive and even though Grandpa Willie returned to Union when I was nine years old, I still did not know him that well.

It was Grandpa Sanders who had a very strong influence on me during my early years. He was the Superintendant of Sunday

School and a deacon at Corinth Baptist Church, and that made him a very important man in the community. Early on in life I came to recognize that the church was the most cherished and important place in our world. Your commitment to God and attendance at church every Sunday was the compass used to measure your moral and ethical worth. If you expected to hold down any position of importance in the community it was mandatory that you attend church; and that we did, every Sunday without fail. Early on Sunday morning the three of us, Marionette my older sister, Grady my younger brother, and I would attend Sunday school, morning worship service and then back in the evening for BTU and the final service.

Reflecting back over my life, I am not convinced that my people could have survived the tragic circumstances under which they lived in a racist and segregated South Carolina without the church. After we lost the battle during the period of Reconstruction for an equal and just society in about 1876, the next hundred years was a nightmare for Black Americans. I was born right in the middle of that nightmare. Just imagine what life was like for our four million ancestors who were set free after the Civil War but were provided with nothing for survival. They received no land, no money, and were confronted with a hostile environment that would have preferred to see them still in bondage and not free. Without the church and their ministers, their faith would have diminished and they may have just given up. But nothing could break their commitment to God and their trust in Jesus Christ. With that as their foundation they endured and that is why I felt very important walking with Grandpa Sanders every Sunday to church. Our minister at Corinth, Reverend Matthew Zimmerman would eventually become my mentor, and once I made the decision to dedicate my life to the ministry, he would become my teacher.

Because of our strong commitment to our church and family, Marionette, Grady and I were very close, and even though Marionette was two years older than me, I often would act like I was the oldest because that was the role the male was expected to assume. But when I would get too far out of line, that is try to flex my tiny muscles, Marionette would remind me that Mama always stressed that she was in charge. She was the oldest and was expected to look out for Grady and me, and keep us out of trouble.

Marionette took her responsibility to watch over us quite

2

seriously. During the years that all three of us attended Macbeth Elementary School together, which was not long since she was five years older than Grady and two older than me, we would walk to school together. On the very hot days she would open her parasol, hold it up over the two of us in order to shade us from the sun. The sun would beat down on her but she never moved that parasol because Mama had told her that she must protect us, and that meant even from the hot sun.

Poppa worked all the time and still had problems making ends meet. He was an excellent painter and was able to find work around Union. But when the jobs dried up in Union, he took jobs out of town that kept him away from home quite a bit. He left early and returned late at night and sometimes would be gone overnight. And for all his time and effort he put into that job, he only made fifteen dollars every two weeks. We were still grateful because the country was locked in a very serious depression, and Black people suffered considerably more than others. Whatever we got was a blessing from God.

In order to subsidize the family income Mama cooked for one white family and then did washing and ironing for four other families. She left out at eight o'clock in the morning and returned home after two in the afternoon. That was her routine six days a week. Many Black women right after slavery cooked in other women's kitchens, washed clothes in other people's washrooms and raised other people's children. Mamma never saw her job as menial and instilled in us at an early age to put forth one hundred percent effort in all that we do.

Because of our parent's work schedule, it was imperative that Nette, Grady, and I work well together which we managed to do without literally killing each other. During school days we got up at six thirty in the morning, prayed, had breakfast, and then headed out to school. We left about the same time as Mama, and she then went in one direction, and the three of us in another. Poppa was already gone when we got up.

On Saturday mornings we got up early and did our assigned chores. Grady and I had the chore of cleaning the outhouse for years; that was a terrible job and I'll never forget the stench and how we tried to squeeze our nose closed while emptying the contents. After all our chores were done, we had some time for play. We did a lot of make believe games. One of our favorites was play-acting a funeral. I acted as the preacher; Marionette was a member of the grieving family, and Grady the undertaker. Early on in life, I was preparing for my future in the ministry. Another make believe game had Grady and I playing the roles of two little pigs. We turned the kitchen chairs on their side and put them in a circle. Grady and I got inside the circle, which was the pigpen. Nette then took four pieces of bread, crumbled them up and soaked them with a water and sugar mixture, and tossed it into our pen. She would then yell "suwee," beckoning the two little pigs to come and eat. We ate the bread using our mouths to scoop it up.

Later in the afternoon we went outside and tossed a soccer sized ball to each other in the front yard. Often the person standing closest to our neighbor's yard, which was usually Grady, would miss the ball and it ended up in our neighbor's yard. By the time we got into their yard to retrieve it, old Mrs. James had run out her front door, grabbed the ball and fussed at us.

"What y'all doin' throwin' this ball in my yard," she scowled.

"Sorry ma'am," I said politely. I always took the lead in situations like this. My chest would swell with pride when I was given the opportunity to converse with adults. Children spoke only when spoken to back then. Young kids never interrupted adult conversations and Heaven forbid they were even in the same room when adults were talking. So the opportunity to talk with Mrs. James was a privilege.

"You kids know you ain't supposed to be throwin' this ball in my yard."

"We didn't mean to," I said. "Grady just missed it when I threw it to him."

"I should tell your mama, but I won't this time."

"Thank you Mrs. James." I reached for the ball and she pulled it in close to her body.

She smiled with a gleam in her eyes. "I tell you what you got to do to get your ball back," she said.

I knew exactly what was coming next. I did an excellent rendition of the hambone. I knew I would have to perform to get the ball back.

"You got to do the hambone for me," she said.

"Yes ma'am."

With both hands open I slapped the outside of my thighs to a rhythmic beat and sang.

"Hambone, hambone, where you been? Round the world and going again." I kept the beat going and sang the words for a couple of minutes.

"Boy, you really know how to do that hambone," Mrs. James said with a smile, then handed me the ball.

"Thank you ma'am." I grabbed the ball and the three of us ran back into our yard and continued playing catch.

Each time I tossed the ball to Grady, I knew there was the possibility that he would miss it and I would again be in Mrs. James's yard doing the hambone all over again.

Mama and Poppa stressed two important things to us as children and that was religion and education. They drilled in our heads that a well-rounded person is one who respects and follows the teachings of Jesus Christ and the teachings of the school. They were inseparable and without both of them we would struggle as adults to make it in a racist society. However, of the two institutions, the church was the most important and dominant. In many ways the function of education was primarily to prepare us for a better understanding of the Bible. The years that I attended Macbeth Elementary School all my teachers were either officials or regular attendees of Corinth, the dominant Black church in Union.

Our school day at Macbeth began with all of us singing a spiritual, and then we had to repeat a number of Bible verses. Mrs. Rose Jackson was my teacher from first grade to the sixth. Macbeth was a converted barn and it housed all the students. When Mrs. Jackson walked in that room you had better be in your seat and be prepared to recite your Biblical verse without the aid of a Bible. If you weren't ready when she called on you, she grabbed her ruler and made the poor victim hold out his or her hand, palms up, and they would get a strong whack. I made sure that every time she got around to me I was ready. That was not the case with my cousin, Harold Young, who lived next door with Grandpa Sanders. Whenever he was called on, he simply said.

"Jesus wept."

I completed grades one through six at Macbeth and then moved on to Sims High School. I attended Sims until I graduated from the eleventh grade. At that time there was no twelfth grade. The years at Sims were the most important in my life. It was during those most formative years that I gave my life to the Lord and I experienced the pleasure of learning under one of the most influential men in South Carolina, Dr. A.A. Sims.

2.

The principal at Sims High School was Dr. A. A. Sims, affectionately called Prof. Sims. He was a very strong, determined, and well-educated man who had the respect of the white community to the extent that was possible. Even though the Union School Board set curriculum and policy for the school, Prof. Sims managed to run that school the way he saw fit.

Prof. Sims was the second most influential Black man in Union. He had taken on the awesome responsibility of educating the young people. Education was second only to religious training during my early years. Blacks throughout the South believed that if the race became educated all kinds of opportunities would open up to them. Our parents looked upon us as the "New Negroes," the generation most removed from the days of slavery when shackles replaced books in the Black man and woman's life. A time when reading was outlawed and using one's mental abilities was unheard of within the world of the slavocracy. But with those times long gone and the opportunity to study and learn about the world that was there for us, most of our parents insisted that we take advantage of it. My parents were no different, and they put me into the hands of Prof. Sims with the assumption that after five years of his tutelage, I would be ready to move onto the next level, which was college.

Prof. Sims was a proud and self-assured man. He told the parents of his students, "Let me have a young man or woman for six months and they'll never plow the cotton fields again." And he did save a large number of young men and women from the cotton fields. Sims High School maintained a high graduation rate.

His approach to education differed vastly from that of the traditional Booker T. Washington Southern model. Whereas Washington dismissed the value of a classical education in favor of a more industrial one, Prof. Sims stressed the importance of studying the classics, to include the Greek philosophers, the English and French writers and the American literary works. Prof. Sims often discussed with us the concept of the "Talented Tenth." He admired Dr. W.E.B. Du Bois, the first Black man to receive a Doctorate Degree from Harvard University and author of *The Soul of Black Folks*, a collection of writings through which he developed the idea that the top ten percent of the race had a responsibility to return to the Black community and educate the other ninety percent. He told us that once we graduated from Sims High School, our next goal must be to graduate from college. After graduation it was our responsibility to return right into the bosom of the race where most of the people were still illiterate, and teach them. That is exactly what he did when he came to Union and set up Sims High School. He welcomed all Black children, to include those who lived outside the city limits and deep in the country where the parents were sharecroppers.

Many of the children had only one pair of overalls and would wear them everyday. That was fine with Prof. Sims but he insisted that they be clean. These children walked miles to get to the school but he also insisted that they be on time. It was unacceptable to be dirty and late. Cleanliness was next to Godliness to Prof. Sims and being late established bad habits, and meant that the student would miss the morning prayer. Besides serving as principal of the school, Prof. Sims was also pastor at Limestone Baptist Church in Gaffney, South Carolina, about twenty miles from Union. Therefore, prayer in the morning was essential for a student to have a productive and meaningful day. Every school morning began with a prayer in your homeroom class.

Like most young people we had our cliques made up of those students who walked to school, shared lunch, and actually studied together. In our case it broke down between the students from Union and those that came in from the countryside. Latta Thomas and I had our own small clique of two. We both had lived in Union all our lives and our interests were similar in that we were committed to getting a college education and teaching.

As young Black men we confronted hardships, as did the entire

Black race. Two particular things irritated Latta and me to no end. The first was that we had old and used hand-me-down books from the white school. They were always torn and raggedy, often with pages missing. One year my history book was filled with caricature drawings of Black people in the cotton fields and one even had a drawing of a Black man hanging from a tree. In the text of these books there was nothing about Nat Turner, Frederick Douglass, Harriet Tubman or Sojourner Truth. No mention was made of the Underground Railroad and the thousands of Black people who refused to succumb to the humiliating effects of slavery. Instead the pages were filled with pictures of happy, smiling and of course dancing men and women with the subtle message that they were content with their station in life. We received a heavy dose of glowing and positive information about Jeff Davis, Robert E. Lee and our most illustrious racist Senator, Ben "Pitchfork" Tillman.

It also angered and irritated us that the white children were provided with buses to take them to and from school while the Blacks had to walk in all kinds of weather. It could be raining or snowing and we still had to walk. Sometimes one of our parents would give us a ride but that didn't happen too often. To add insult to injury, when the white children passed us on the bus they yelled racial epithets and threw objects at us. Given the nature of the southern system we dare not retaliate. We constantly were ducking apple cords, banana peelings and one time Latta was hit with a baseball. But there was nothing we could do.

My favorite classes in high school were those taught by Prof. Sims. He made class exciting and interesting by telling stories about his experiences with racism, and the color caste system within the Black community. One of the more interesting stories he told was about one of his early experiences with the color issue at the school. When he first taught elementary school in Union, it was a rule that you did not whip the light skinned children. It was perfectly acceptable to whip those of a darker hue. He had one light skinned student who loved to flaunt his skin color as a badge of privilege. He knew he could not be whipped regardless of what he did in class.

As the boy's classroom behavior worsened, Prof. Sims finally decided he would not tolerate the boy's obstinacy any longer. He clearly understood the rule but after a while it did not matter to him. To the shock of the entire class, he called the boy to the front of the room, bent him over and gave him a swift, smooth blow to the buttocks. The boy let out a loud yelp and ran out of the classroom. The class, and especially the darker students, got a great deal of pleasure and appreciated the fact that Prof. Sims was going to be an equal opportunity dispenser of blows to the buttocks of any student who dared challenge his authority in the classroom. Early on in high school I understood his non-discriminatory policy and gave him no reason to introduce his swing to my hind side.

Prof. Sims employed the carrot and stick approach to encourage his students to work hard in the classroom. On any given day he would stroll into the classroom and begin.

"Young people, someday the Black man will rule the world; for we are descendants of great rulers and leaders. Our forefathers are the great Solomon and Hannibal, and our mothers descend from Queen of Sheba and many other great ladies."

Prof. Sims not only used historical examples but contemporary ones also. "Our race has numerous examples of scholars and athletes that today are excelling in their fields of endeavor. One of the greatest scholars is Dr. W.E.B. Du Bois, one of the founders of the National Association of Colored People and a great writer and philosopher. In sports we have two of the greatest heavyweight world champions in Jack Johnson and today Joe Louis. We all remember his great victory over the so-called invincible German fighter Max Schmelling."

The mention of the Louis victory brought back memories and I began to daydream about that day. I was nine years old at the time and even though it had been years past, I distinctly remember all the details. The "Brown Bomber" was a native son of the South; the son of Alabama cotton pickers. Joe Louis had the entire country in an excited frenzy when he fought Schmelling in a rematch on June 22, 1938, after losing to him before. Grandpa was the only person in the neighborhood who owned a radio and Black folk crowded into his home to hear the fight. It was an extremely hot day but that didn't matter; no one was going to miss listening to the fight. Mamma and Poppa, along with most of the adults from church, had gotten off early. The women made Sunday dinner on a Wednesday and our kitchen was filled with wonderful aromas. They brought fried chicken, greens, okra, potato salad, crackling bread, corn bread, buttermilk biscuits and sweet potato pie.

Mamma and the ladies spread the checkerboard table cloths on the tables set up by the men in the yard. The ladies prepared the food and the men all gathered in the living room to listen to the fight. Folks were scurrying in and out of the house, talking about the fight and how they knew Louis would win this time.

Finally when Clem McCarthy the broadcaster began to talk, the room was instantly silent. That is when I knew this event was important.

"Left jab from Louis to Schmelling's midsection, now a right jab to his jaw," McCarthy announced in his crushed gravel sounding voice. The way he rolled his r's was electrifying to hear.

"Yeah, all right," the men inside shouted.

"Louis lands another right to Schmelling's jaw and it staggered the German," McCarthy's voice rose a couple decibels. "Another right to the head and a left to the mid-section. Schmelling is putting up no defense. It won't be long now."

The women who had been outside, stopped what they were doing, ran up to the front door and gathered there to listen. From the commotion inside they knew something was about to happen. Finally, the house exploded when McCarthy shouted.

"Schmelling is down. The count is five, six, seven, eight, nine, the fight is over. Joe Louis has knocked Schmelling out in the first round. The heavyweight championship is coming back to the United States."

"We won, we won," Poppa shouted, then he and his friends jumped up and down.

Joe Louis had made Black Americans joyous and proud. From those standing outside Yankee Stadium listening to the fight, to the artists and writers in Harlem, to the newly transplanted Blacks in Chicago, to Black men working on chain gangs and the railroads, to those in all parts of South Carolina. Louis helped simple men dream again, and dream for me and my generation.

Grandpa sat quietly in his favorite chair in the corner of the room and cried silently. Mamma's face turned red from crying as she told Marionette, Grady and me, "this is a great day for all Negroes, we won today." I did not know the full meaning of what had just happened but I cried because we had won.

"Yes, Joe knocked that man out in the first round." Prof. Sims was on a roll as he continued to point out the greatness in our race.

Almost instantaneously, my mind wandered back to the lesson being given by Prof. Sims. I scolded myself because I dare not daydream and reminisce too long. If I was caught not listening, I would surely be a victim of the paddle. I honed in on what he was saying just as he took in a deep breath, released it and smiled. He continued.

"Then just a few years before Louis, Jesse Owens beat those so-called superior German athletes in the 1936 Olympics. So young men begin your work for the day knowing that you will someday be the leaders of this great nation, and will ultimately make it greater than what it is now." That was the carrot approach and then there was the stick whenever he felt we were not attentive.

He did not stroll into the classroom but instead barged in.

"A bunch of shiftless, lazy Negroes, that is exactly what you all are going to be in life. You all have no ambition or no desire to succeed and as a result you will get exactly what you deserve, and that is nothing. A bunch of useless Negroes have never amounted to anything and never will." His eyebrows furrowed.

Our initial response was anger. How dare he talk to us in that manner? How dare he demean an entire race because of the few? But it also stimulated us to work harder on that particular day. I don't care what the subject, we were determined to complete all our assignments. We usually did, and at the end of the day we still had the utmost respect for the man.

Not only did the students admire Prof. Sims, but he was also a hero in the community. He was known as a Black man who did not back down to the white harassment. As part of the "New Negro" generation, the young people in Prof. Sims' classes were proud to know he didn't walk around with that old slave mentality. Our chests stuck out when he told of his confrontation with a white man who came up to him and said,

"Sims, I hear that Pruitt has passed away." Dr. Pruitt was a great Black educator in the state of Alabama.

"Yes, unfortunately Pruitt is gone," Prof. Sims, replied.

At that point he assumed the discussion was over. After all, white men hardly ever carried on prolonged discussions with Blacks. That was considered beneath them and if observed by other whites, it could be reason to be ridiculed. But this time, the white man wanted to make an additional point.

"You people ought to build a monument to that man," he said. "Not only would he tip his hat to a white woman, he would also tip his hat to white men. Yes, he was a good ole boy who knew his place."

Prof. Sims stared at the man for a few seconds and then retorted. "Then it seems to me that you folks are the ones that ought to build the monument." He finished, then turned and walked away from the man.

Prof. Sims laughed and told us that the man refused to speak to him for over six months. But he also admonished us that his response was not always the wisest one. Negroes had been beaten and even lynched for lesser offenses against white folks.

He advised us to concentrate on accomplishing a better life than what our parents experienced. Prof. Sims believed that with each generation conditions would improve. He then would pull out a self-help manual, published in Atlanta, Georgia in 1905. The small manual was titled, *Floyd's Flowers or Duty and Beauty for Colored Children*. The advice in that manual had served young Blacks for years. He would read the most important passage to us.

"I believe that the less you think about the troubles of the race and the less you talk about them and the more time you spend in hard and honest works, believing in God and trusting Him for the future, the better it will be for all concerned."

Prof. Sims didn't suggest that we take abuse from white people but only that we not concentrate on their abusive nature. He would explain that they are also the victims of an unfair system. They had been taught to believe that there was something intrinsically good and beautiful being white, whereas in reality there really was no difference in the races. But since the odds were so overwhelmingly against us, we should only concentrate on those things that we can affect in a positive way. I have no doubt that his advice was based on his fear of violence against us if we spoke out against the inequities our people suffered in the 1940's. But we were the young people who would within twenty years reject that thinking. We were the young generation who were being trained to take on the challenges of the 1960's, and fight against an evil system that had destroyed so many of our people over the decades here in this country.

Besides Prof. Sims, my other favorite high school teacher was Cyrus Williams. Black folks in Union called him Psyche Williams. I never knew exactly why they gave him that name unless it was because he always seemed to be off in deep thought. Mr. Williams was another Black man who refused to succumb to the racism of the times. Like Prof. Sims, he also had a direct confrontation with racism and did not accept the silly nonsense that Blacks were inferior.

The story spread around the school that one day Mr. Williams went into the Five and Dime store to make a purchase. When he found the items he wanted to buy, he got in a long line leading up to the counter. Once he reached the counter the young white female clerk said.

"And now what can I do for you, Uncle?'

Mr. Williams stared at her for a moment and said.

"Young lady if your mother kept this secret all these years that I was her brother, why did you have to go and break it?" With that said, he turned around and walked out of the store, leaving the item he planned to purchase on the counter.

What we found most sickening about segregation occurred during the war years. I was in my second year at Sims High School when the United States Army began to march German prisoners through Union. Initially, the prisoners were stationed at Camp Croft in Spartanburg, and then moved down to Fort Jackson in Columbia, their final destination. On their way to Columbia they stopped in Union to eat. The German prisoners were allowed to eat in the local cafeteria, while the Black citizens had to get their food from an opening on the side of the building. If you wanted a hamburger, you would stick your money through the opening, and when the hamburger was ready, the person inside would hand it to you. Blacks were not allowed inside the restaurant, and that included Black soldiers fighting to protect America's democracy.

14

The Life of Reverend James W. Sanders

One of the many tragedies of the south was that German soldiers were more valued than Black American soldiers returning from war. Many of them would be labeled "uppity" when they returned and insisted on equal treatment. Some were even hanged in their uniforms.

As students we were irate and questioned Prof. Sims as to why should Black men go and fight for a country that treated its enemies better than its own citizens. Prof. Sims stared at us for a long while before replying. He knew what he said would affect the manner in which we viewed this country in the future, so he was contemplative in his answer. Finally this very staid man said,.

"There have been two sides to this argument regarding our involvement in a war for a country that has failed to give us the rights that others enjoy. There are those like A. Phillip Randolph, a great union man, who argues that we should refuse to fight. In fact, he is willing to go to jail in opposition to the war. So is his assistant, Bayard Rustin."

I glared over at Latta and he looked at me also. We both had quizzical expressions because we did not know who these two men were. I jotted down both their names, determined to find out more about them on my own. I then turned my attention back to Prof. Sims.

"And then there are leaders who have encouraged us to put our differences aside and fight to defend our country. Among these men you'll find Walter White of the NAACP, and also Dr. W.E.B. Du Bois, although Dr. Du Bois is not as enthusiastic about our participation in this war as he was the first one. Evidently, when this country failed to live up to its promise to bring the same kind of democracy to the United States as they brought in the liberation of France, Russia and England, Dr. Du Bois was quite disappointed. But he does not take as strong a stand against the war as Mr. Randolph."

"What is your position, Prof. Sims?" I asked.

Again he hesitated before answering. Finally he said.

"These people argue that we should not be allowed to fight in the war. They wanted us in the army but only as cooks and to clean their clothes and shine their boots. In fact, there is a group of young Negro men down at Tuskegee who have trained to be pilots but the politicians don't want to let them fly because it might destroy their lie that our boys are not brave enough, and don't have the ability to fly dangerous flights over enemy territory. But we all know better. Truth in the matter is that those young Negroes can out fly all those white men put together. So, despite all the problems with this country, I believe our boys should go and prove to all these people that they can fight, and often better than any other race of people." He paused as if to assess how his comments affected us. "But this way of treating our people must stop," he continued as his voice rose a couple decibels. "And it will be up to young men of this generation to force that change. Some of you sitting right in this room will be at the forefront of that change. So we can endure just a little bit longer. We know God is on our side, and just as He brought an end to slavery, He will put an end to this nonsense."

One of the most important lessons both Prof. Sims, Mr. Williams and most of our teachers at Sims High taught us was how we had an obligation to the race and culture to complete our education. We were told stories passed down by generations, but never mentioned in our history books, of the horrors our ancestors confronted after the Civil War for simply trying to go to school. We listened almost in shock as he told of schools being burned down, and teachers pulled out of their homes and beaten because they dared to teach our ancestors how to read and write. It was with an extreme sense of pride that I related to men and women, even in their later lives, who if they couldn't read, made sure their children, could.

If the white school board had gotten wind of some of the history Prof. Sims and Mr. Williams taught us behind the closed doors of Sims High School, they probably would have fired them and possibly ran them out of town. They were brave men but they would always tells us that they were led by God, and with Him on their side they didn't have to worry. By the age fifteen, I knew that I wanted to be a God fearing man just like the men in my life, to include Grandpa Sanders, Daddy, Prof. Sims and Mr. Williams. I also decided that I would enter the ministry and continue the great works that God had led these men to do. I only needed to wait for God to deliver my calling to me, and that happened soon after I made the decision to dedicate my life to Him .

3.

"James Sanders, get in this building right now."

I heard Prof. Sims' voice call out to me as I stood right next to the fence that surrounded the school yard. The other students had gone inside at the end of recess but for some reason I felt compelled to remain behind. Something was pulling at me and the force was so powerful I couldn't resist. I had a feeling of discovering nature for the very first time. I stared at a ladybug in the grass, reached down and picked it up. Momentarily my mind slipped away from my instructor's orders to return to the classroom. I had never disobeyed an order from Prof. Sims or any of my teachers, but this invisible but audible pull was much greater than any one teacher and in fact greater than all of them together. My eyes and thoughts concentrated on that very small bug and all its secrets. It was created and it survived because of the master of the universe.

I stared up at the sky. The force became more powerful than before. I began to cry, not out of sadness but true joy that resonated from deep inside my soul. My entire body was engulfed with a feeling that made me want to both shout out in joy and cry in jubilation because the passion was so overwhelmingly positive. Not tears of sorrow or despair but only jubilation. I suddenly recognized the change that had grabbed me and refused to let go. I couldn't have turned and walked back into the school if I wanted to. As a fifteen-year-old Black boy, I felt a distinct love and it was for the Lord and his son Jesus Christ, my savior. He died for me and He loved all mankind so much that He went to the cross to take away all our sins and shame. I knew then I had been called to serve Jesus from that day on.

"James Sanders I'm going to give you one more minute to get back into this classroom or you're going to get five good swats." Prof. Sims again called out.

Finally realizing what had just happened I smiled, turned and ran back into the school building. As I shot past Prof. Sims I said.

"Sorry sir, but I really need to talk with you after school."

"It better be awfully important," he scowled, closed the door and we returned to the classroom.

Later that afternoon when our final class for the day was over, I told Latta that I wouldn't be walking home with him, but had to meet with Prof. Sims.

"Yeah, you have to explain what happened this morning, don't you?" He asked

"Not really but yes really I do."

Latta glared at me. "You all right?"

"Better than I have ever been," I said. "I'll tell you all about it later but first I have to know it's real."

"Okay, talk to you later," he said, turned and left the building

As I strolled down the hallway toward Prof. Sims' office I was nervous, almost to the point of panicking. God didn't directly talk to me like He did with prophets in the Old Testament, but the feeling that took control of my entire body was His sending the Holy Ghost to tell me it was time. I was nervous because I had to share this information with Prof. Sims and could only hope that he would know what I had experienced, since I assumed he had experienced a similar feeling when he received his calling.

I had been feeling the tug at my heart for the past few weeks. When I went to the hotel where I worked as a bus boy and a waiter, I heard the voice of Jesus. My brother Grady and his friends had come by the hotel wanting me to go with them to visit a few young ladies. The voice told me, "No, you are in this world, but not of this world." I prayed that Prof. Sims would understand what I was experiencing.

A renewed exuberance shot through my body as I sank down in one of the plush leather chairs in front of Prof. Sims' large oak desk. I was overwhelmed by the ambiance of his office. His walls were covered with the many awards and plaques he had received over the years. But the most impressive award of all hung right in the middle of all the others and that was his Doctorate Degree Certificate. It read in large black letters; "THE BOARD OF REGENTS OF ST. PAUL UNIVERSITY CONFER ON A.A. SIMS THE DEGREE DOCTORATE OF PHILOSOPHY, MAY 13, 1936." Each time I had the opportunity to read those words it increased my determination to someday have the same degree as the man who served as one of my role models.

I sat quietly waiting for Prof. Sims to speak first. I wondered what words would come to me and how I would explain what I experienced earlier in the schoolyard. He never looked up when I sat down, but instead his eyes remained glued to some document in front of him. His inattention to me actually gave me time to get my thoughts together. If what I had experienced earlier was my calling to preach then there was no reason for me to be nervous. I was now a vessel of God, and He would provide me with the right words to explain this new revelation in my life.

"What is it James?"

Prof. Sims brought me out of my musing. Now it was my turn.

"Earlier this afternoon, I truly believe that I received my calling to do the Lord's work," I said without stumbling over my words. "What I wanted to find out from you is did you have a similar experience when you received your calling?"

Prof. Sims gave me a hard and long stare as if to let me know that I should never make such a comparison to him. After all I was only fifteen years old. But when he finally spoke that was not the case at all.

"Yes I did and it was about at the same age as you. Any sincerely blessed servant of God who has been called to preach the word must go to through that same experience. If a preacher tells you that he has not been brought to tears because of the joy he felt when the Lord called him to do His work, then you know you are talking to a pretender, a false prophet. Congratulations, James." He paused, drew in a deep breath and released it. "You must now begin your studies," he continued, "but first you must sit with your parents and with your Grandfather and let them know what has happened in your life. Let them know that you are now a special child of God, a new disciple of Jesus, and that He will direct your life from this time on. Explain to them that you will still be obedient to them but your first obedience is to God. They will understand."

"Yes sir."

"Your pastor is Reverend Zimmerman, so it is just as important that you begin your studies under him. But you must also make sure that you stay on top of your studies here at the school. You now have two major responsibilities, and that is to your formal education and then to your future ministry. Both will demand a great deal of your time. You will have very little time for other endeavors. Keep your mind on your prize. You are one of God's gifted children and a lot will be expected of you." Prof. Sims smiled and stood up.

"Yes sir."

He now did something I'd never known him to do with students. He walked to the other side of his desk and sat in the empty chair next to me. He leaned toward me and continued.

"James, you are about to take on an awesome responsibility." His voice softened. "Please never take it lightly. We are still a rather illiterate people. No fault of our own, but it is true. The only thing many of our people have is the trust and faith in God. They believe He will deliver them someday, just as their ancestors believed that He would deliver them from bondage. When you finish your studies and when you get your first church, do not let your people down. Be the best minister you possibly can be."

"Yes sir."

Prof. Sims stood up. "Now it's time for you to go and share this good news with your father and mother. And you must see Reverend Zimmerman to begin your studies. But in the meantime, I expect to see you in class bright and early, ready to continue your academic studies."

"Yes sir." I also stood up and prepared to leave.

"See you in the morning and welcome to the world of Jesus, the Holy Spirit, and our Father in Heaven."

No further words were necessary. I just smiled and nodded obediently. It seemed as if Prof. Sims had tears in his eyes as well. The contemplative stare that my mentor gave me was one of patriarchal pride. A soul-searching look that communicated to me that his job was complete because he saw the leadership in me. He knew my classmates and I would take the torch and run with it in the future. I turned and left his office.

Prof. Sims' affirmation that my calling was real and that all ministers, who receive a similar calling, also have a similar awakening is exactly what I needed to hear. I practically ran out of the school building and up the street. I had to hurry home and share my joy with Mama and Poppa. No doubt they would be thrilled to learn that their oldest son now had something in common with the great ministers of our race, to include Reverend Zimmerman. Someday I would be as great as the best and most renowned ministers that lived and preached in South Carolina. That was a lofty goal but one I knew, God willing, I could accomplish. My mind was in a fog and before I knew it, I rushed up the porch steps and through the front door of our home.

"James why are you late getting home from school?" Mama asked as I threw my books in the bedroom and hurried into the kitchen where she was preparing supper. The smell of fat back in the cast iron skillet made my mouth water. Nette stood next to Mama stirring corn meal into the boiling water. Mama turned around and poured the fat back grease into another cast iron skillet. I knew they were making Johnny cake.

Grady ran into kitchen. He had been next door listening to the radio with Grandpa. He could hardly contain himself. "Mama, President Roosevelt announced that all the soldiers going to be able to go to college for nothing and they going to be able to get loans from the government to buy homes and farms."

"Grady, I appreciate you trying to impress me with all these current events, but if you're going to ask me can you hang out on the street corner after dinner, the answer is no."

Nette and I smiled. Mama could read all three of us like a book. But what I had to tell her was more important than something the president was doing or Grady hanging out on the corner. It was my turn.

"Mama, I have to talk to you and Poppa," I said.

"What's got you so excited?" Mama asked.

"What I have to tell you has to be with Poppa present."

"Boy, are you in some kind of trouble?"

"No Mama, nothing like that."

"All right then, your Poppa will be here about seven. He had a job over in Gaffney and should be on his way back soon. We'll all talk after dinner, that is, if he isn't too tired. In the meantime, I know you have some homework so get on it, right now."

"Yes Mama," I said and headed back to my bedroom. I was confident that Poppa wouldn't be too tired to listen, after all this entire situation was being orchestrated by God.

Poppa always sat at the head of the table, Nette and Mamma on one side and Grady and I on the other side. We all had loaded our plates with collard greens, fat back, slab bacon and Johnny cake. Sweet potato pie sat at the end of the table waiting to be cut once we finished our main meal.

During dinner neither Mama or Poppa asked why I needed to talk to them. Instead their conversation was about George Stinney, a young boy who we all knew. It was a sad situation but not unfamiliar to Negroes in the south.

"George's parents came by Daddy's house today after it was all over," Poppa said. "Seems as though our petition did no good at all."

"Did you think it would?" Mama asked

"No, not really. When those folks decide they going to kill a Negro they just do it." Poppa took in a fork full of greens.

Poppa had kept the news from us because of the fear it would have caused. But now they were discussing it freely. George Stinney, only 14 years old, had been executed in the electric chair for the alleged killing of two white girls who were eight and eleven. His parents had been run out of town so he had to stand trial with an all white jury, and no family support. Right after he was arrested, a mob showed up at the jail and wanted to lynch him. The sheriff fought them off but assured the mob that he would get his just due in court, He got what they considered his just due. He was electrocuted.

"That boy was so tiny, only ninety pounds and not even five feet tall. And they put him in the electric chair." Mama's eyes filled up with tears.

"Clarendon County sent that boy to Columbia to be executed just like a dog," Poppa scowled.

Poppa and Mama suddenly stopped talking and just continued to eat. The silence was deafening. How could those people do that to a boy only fourteen? I was his age and that could have been me or Grady, God forbid, Nette. I felt both fear and anger. I knew there were unbelievable injustices and cruelty against Negroes but this was personal to me and far more so than ever before, I felt that I must commit my life, through Christ, to fight injustices. As much as I wanted to shout out my good news right at the table, I refrained. It was not the right time and Poppa had a process for discussing family matters.

"Nette and Grady, clear off these dishes and then go do your homework," Mama said. "James needs to talk with your Poppa and me in private."

I wanted to shout out to them to hurry up because I was about to burst out of my britches with excitement. Nette and Grady got up, cleared the table and disappeared into their bedrooms. Poppa, Mama and I stayed around the table.

Usually family meetings took place in the living room and depending on the nature of the subject the entire family would be there to participate in the discussion. One time Poppa called a family meeting to discuss his involvement in a crisis situation that could have possibly gotten him killed. There was a Negro man who had run off up North with his white girlfriend and got married. Knowing that mixed marriages were illegal in South Carolina, they still returned to Union. When the city officials found out they were back in town they set out to find them, and probably lynch the Black man. Poppa allowed them to stay with us for a couple days and then helped them escape. He explained to us that men and women had to take a stand for what was just and right. Two people in love should not be persecuted because of racist laws. Poppa was gone the entire night, and we all were relieved when he finally got home the next day.

On another occasion we had a family meeting to discuss Nette's going off to college. Poppa explained to Grady and me that he could not afford to pay all her expenses, and that we would have to work to help her out. He promised us that when it was our turn to go off to college and she was settled into a job, she would then assist us. Grady and I went to work for Mr. Chalk who owned a cleaners that served people in the city as well as the rural areas. I would drive the owner's car up to the house where we had to pick up the dirty clothes, Grady would jump out of the car, run up to the house and get the clothes. We gladly did that in order to help our sister. And it was all a result of a family meeting in the living room.

Then there was the time that Poppa decided to run for city council in Union. That was unheard of for a Black man, but like his daddy, he feared no man or any situation. We had a family discussion and he threw his hat in the ring. Quite naturally he lost but I admired him for trying. That decision he made was also the result of a family discussion.

However, the most interesting of all the family discussions occurred when Poppa called us together to explain the heroics of Grandpa Sanders. We were told that Grandpa's younger brother was about to be lynched by a white mob for looking at a white woman the wrong way. Some friends rushed to Grandpa's house and told him what was happening. Grandpa shot out of the house and hurried up to the towns square. He confronted the mob, grabbed his brother by the arm and marched him right by the angry men and to his home. For a while we weren't sure what would be the repercussions and Poppa wanted us to stay close to the house when not at school in case there would be trouble. There wasn't any and Grandpa got away with an act that would possibly have gotten his brother and him lynched. And we found out about it at a family meeting. Now it was time for them to find out about me in the same kind of meeting, but without Grady and Nette.

"Your Mama said you came running in this house like some kind of crazy boy," Poppa began the discussion.

"Yes sir," I concurred in his assessment.

"So what is so important that you got in late from school and now you asked for a family conference?" He asked.

"Poppa, this morning I received my calling to the ministry," I blurted out. "God called me to be His teacher down here and to be a disciple to Christ." The words rolled off my tongue with ease. God was in charge and I was His vehicle.

"Oh blessed be His holy name. Thank you Jesus," Mama chimed in.

"Are you sure this is what you want to do?" Poppa asked.

"It's not what I want to do, it's what God has chosen me to do," I answered politely. I didn't want to sound curt talking to Poppa, but the words just came naturally.

"Then let me explain to you that in order to serve our community you must serve as a beacon of light for our future. Our people look to the minister to give them guidance and hope. They also expect our ministers to be beyond reproach. You bring disgrace on your family and on you if you cannot live up to the very high standards that your followers will expect."

"Yes son, if you're going to be a preacher, let your behavior reflect God's presence in your life, and don't be no jack legged preacher," Mama snuck in her comments while Poppa paused to take a drink of water out of his favorite mason jar.

"There are only a few Professions open to our educated men. One is teaching, being a barber or an undertaker and of course the ministry." A big smile crossed Poppa's face. "Let me tell you a joke going around about some of these so-called preachers. It goes like this. A man was out in the cotton field on a very hot day in Alabama. He looked at the long rows of cotton then stared up at the hot sun and said, ' That's a whole lot of rows of cotton, that's a whole lot of heat from the sun and that's a whole lot of work I ain't interested in doing.' The man tossed the cotton sack to the side, walked out of the field and announced that 'I jest got my callin' to the ministry.'

Mama and Poppa broke out in laughter. I even managed a smile. Poppa then got up and stood in front of me. "I'm proud of you son and we know you will be the very best that God has promised you. Now I believe it's time to get your Grandpa and the three of us go over to the church to meet with Reverend Zimmerman."

Grandpa was elated when we gave him the news. It was a little after seven o'clock but he insisted that we go immediately to the church. Tuesday night was prayer night and Reverend Zimmerman would be there to administer prayer to anyone who needed it. For years Grandpa had been a deacon at the church as well as Superintendent of Sunday school. There was no question that I would study ministry at a Baptist church, specifically at Corinth and under Reverend Zimmerman. Grandpa respected Reverend Zimmerman but sometimes felt he was a little too condescending to the system.

One time Reverend Zimmerman was preaching a funeral at Corinth and some white folks came into the church. They automatically walked to the front pews and many of the Blacks got up, gave them their seats and went to the back of the church. Grandpa was irate. He jumped from his pew, went to the back of the church and insisted that the members return to the front. They did not and Reverend Zimmerman said nothing. Grandpa stayed angry for a long time but, for the most part, he thought a lot of our pastor and was determined that I would study under his tutelage.

After prayer meeting was over we followed Reverend Zimmerman to his office in the back of the church. He sat behind his big oak desk, Poppa and Grandpa sat in the chairs in front of the desk, and I sat on a large leather couch on the side of the room. Grandpa controlled the conversation.

"Reverend, God has just delivered to me one of the greatest blessings I could have ever gotten from Him. He has placed a calling on my grandson, James."

"Praise the Lord, that is a blessing for you and your family," Reverend Zimmerman said. "But you have always led your family down the right road to salvation and now God has given you the greatest blessing He could ever give to a family. To be a disciple for Jesus assures your salvation here on earth. You all are already saved by the blood of Jesus Christ and now your grandson will take up the responsibility to deliver God's children to that same salvation you now enjoy."

"You know he must study here at Corinth and he must study under you," Grandpa said.

"It would be my honor to train him."

The Life of Reverend James W. Sanders

They carried on a conversation just like I was not in the room. I thought maybe Reverend Zimmerman would at least look in my direction and ask me a few questions, but this was the custom and the rules. Aside from the fact that I was the person who had just been called to the ministry, in their eyes I was a child and in Black Southern culture children were to be seen and not heard. I was content to sit there and listen to men whom I really respected. I thought how fortunate I was to have such strong and powerful role models in my life. In that one day I had discussed my future with Prof. Sims my educational mentor, with Poppa and Grandpa, my two mentors on life itself, and Reverend Zimmerman, who was my religious mentor.

While they continued to discuss the particulars of my training, my mind wandered back to a book Prof. Sims required us to read. Dr. W.E.B. Du Bois had written a series of essays titled, *The Souls of Black Folks*. Dr. Du Bois was the pre-eminent scholar and the titular head of the Black race. I am not sure the white school board had approved the use of his book in our class, but Prof. Sims had us read it. There was one section in the book that discussed the concept of the "Talented Tenth." In 1903, the year Dr. Du Bois made his observations; the majority of the race was still illiterate. Having been out of slavery for only thirty-eight years, there was no way they could have achieved a literacy level commensurate with the white world. But he argued that there was at least ten percent of the race that were capable of achieving high academic standards. This ten percent should then go to college, study the classics, history, math, and science, then return back to the Black community and teach the other ninety percent, so at a point in time the entire race would be literate.

As I listened to these three wise men I knew I was in the presence of the talented tenth and I said a short prayer thanking God for my position and place in life with them.

< The Spiritual Journey of a Legend >

4.

As usual, on Sunday morning Corinth was packed and we sat in our usual place right behind the deacons. Grandpa was the Chairman of the Deacon Board and Poppa had just become a deacon the previous year. They sat in the front row. To be able to sit right up front, the closest to Reverend Zimmerman, was an honor and the men wore it as a badge of distinction. Wives and family members of the deacons, with the first lady sat in the second row. Reverend Zimmerman, along with Reverend A. C. Duncan, who would be the guest speaker for the day, sat in large leather chairs behind the pulpit. Behind them stood the twenty-member choir. They had brought the church to its feet with their beautiful rendition of "Fire in my Bones."

The lead singer bellowed out,

"I feel fire all shut up in my bones.

Like Jeremiah, it won't let me alone.

I'm going to sing till the almighty power comes around

Spirit got me so I can't sit down."

Before the choir finished and sat down, the entire congregation had jumped to their feet and with arms swinging and hands clapping joined in the joy of the moment. I sat there with a great deal of anxiety because Reverend Zimmerman had told me, during Sunday school, that he wanted to talk with me after the service. I had no idea what he was going to say to me. Maybe he was going to tell me that he had second thoughts and that he didn't feel I was fit for the ministry. Maybe he was going to suggest that I study under Reverend Duncan. I just knew he was going to get us together right after the service and turn me over to this man who was a giant among preachers. He was President of the PACOLET Baptist Association, the association of all the Baptist Ministers in Union and surrounding areas. He was also the father of my friend Malachi Duncan, who at that time was off fighting in the war for the country. Malachi, nine years older than me, would often escort me to Macbeth Elementary School on his way to Sims High. All these thoughts shot through my mind like a speeding bullet as the choir finally finished "Precious Lord Take my Hand," and the guest speaker stood before us and began his sermon.

Of all the ministers I had heard, none of them preached the word of the Lord quite the way Reverend A. C. Duncan did. He could light up a church. There was no sleeping during his sermon unless you were practically dead. In fact the word was that he could raise the dead because of the power of his delivery. I listened intently as he preached about "Job" and the suffering he endured but at the end of his endurance he received the greatest of all rewards and that was blessings from the Lord. Reverend Duncan talked about the suffering of our people right in the state of South Carolina and in Union. His voice raised a couple decibels as he stressed the point that we are under the test of God and because we endure right now, soon we would have victory over evil men and evil deeds.

Reverend Duncan warmed up to the occasion. He took off his suit coat and vest, rolled up his sleeves and really leaned into his sermon. He preached that we must never waver in our faith and always put our problems in the hands of the Lord. But he also told the congregation that the Lord helps the man who helps himself. It was important that we all get as much education as possible, and we read regularly and keep up with world events.

"Children, a change is coming here in the South," he preached. "We must be prepared to take advantage of those changes. Our people are about to be delivered from oppression just like God delivered the Jews out of Egypt. He is preparing to open up another Red Sea and let his people pass through to freedom." He paused, pulled a white handkerchief from his pocket and wiped his forehead. He then sipped from a glass of water next to him. "And just like God delivered Moses to lead His chosen people, He is going to deliver a leader to lead the Negroes, God's chosen people, from bondage. We must be prepared for that day."

What a powerful preacher, I thought mesmerized by this man's delivery. Excitement soared throughout my entire body as I imagined me standing before a congregation, delivering a powerful message from God. At that moment I knew I must study hard and learn every aspect of the Bible and be able to put together sermons that could touch the very soul of my people. The key to any preacher was to deliver the word that there was hope for all of us, and that hope could be found in the words of God and His son Jesus Christ. The joy exuding from the congregation as this man gave them hope touched everyone in the sanctuary. Some waved their arms in agreement, some shouted, "hallelujah," and others jumped to their feet and let the spirit take over. The entire sermon was therapeutic for people who needed the church in order to deal with life. How else could they endure the insults, the lies, the ugliness, and even the lynching of their loved ones without the Lord? It was very clear to me that they couldn't. As Reverend Duncan brought his sermon to an end I was more than willing to accept the responsibility God had placed on me in the schoolyard.

Reverend Zimmerman ended the service with a call to anyone who needed a church home to come forward and join Corinth. Grandpa and Poppa stood up in front of the congregation anxious to greet anyone who might need help making it down the aisle to join. The choir sang:*"Hallelujah to the King,"* softly in the background as Reverend Zimmerman encouraged the unsaved to come forward and be saved.

"If you desire a church come forward and let us greet you into the house of the Lord," he said. He held his arms straight out as a gesture for those who needed God in their lives to come forward. "I want everyone to please bow your heads and close your eyes, and those of you who feel reluctant to come forward can then come down that middle aisle, and turn your life around."

I followed his instructions. I bowed my head and closed my eyes. He continued to urge any one in the congregation to come forward. Reverend Zimmerman had a very unique way of making everyone feel comfortable, and that they were among friends. At that moment I knew I would study his technique carefully and use it once I got a church. It worked because when he finally instructed us to lift our heads and open our eyes, five people stood up front ready to give their lives to Jesus Christ.

Reverend Zimmerman and Duncan came down from behind the pulpit and shook hands with the five new members. Poppa then led those five to a side door, and out of the sanctuary. From his place in the middle aisle, Reverend Zimmerman dismissed the church. As all the others filed out to the back, I strolled over to where he and Reverend Duncan stood. There was a long line of members standing there also. While some congratulated Reverend Duncan on a great sermon, others just wanted to shake his hand. I waited my turn and finally stood in front of these two great men quite nervous for what they would say.

"James, I wanted to tell you in front of Reverend Duncan, a man I know you respect and admire, that it would be my privilege to train you in the ministry," Reverend Zimmerman said.

At that moment I felt a burden lifted from me. But not sure how I should respond, I listened.

"Let me assure you, young man, you have one of the best teachers in the entire state of South Carolina," Reverend Duncan added. "But it is imperative that you must find a way to balance your religious teachings with your school work. They go hand in hand."

"Yes sir, I understand." I noticed Grandpa standing off to the side. No doubt he was proud as he watched two great men advise his grandson. "I understand that most of my time will now be dedicated to my studies and I am prepared to make that sacrifice."

"Yes, it will be very difficult for you," Reverend Zimmerman said. "I was just a little older than you when I started my ministry in Rock Hill, and I was also already in junior college. You're younger and not as mature as I was when I received my calling. But through hard work, and with the help of your father and grandfather, and of course the good Lord, I'll get you through. Tomorrow after school we get started. Be here at four o'clock sharp and we'll begin."

"Thank you, sir," I said.

"You may go," Reverend Zimmerman said. He and Reverend Duncan turned and walked toward the side door leading to the church office.

I also turned and looked at Grandpa who was all smiles. I strolled over to him and said.

"I begin my training in the morning."

"Are you excited?" He asked and wrapped his arms around my shoulder.

"Yes, Grandpa," I said. "Excited and a little scared."

"Scared about what?" He smiled with a sense of pride.

"That I won't be able to live up to the high standard that men like Reverend Duncan, Reverend Zimmerman, you and Poppa have set."

"James, that is why we set a high standard so that you and other young men will have something to strive toward. Set your goals higher and higher until you reach the top. You will be the best minister the state of South Carolina ever produced."

With his arms still tightly wrapped around me, we strolled out of the church and joined the rest of the family waiting for us. That Sunday dinner was one of the best Mama ever prepared. She claimed it was done as a celebration of my commitment to do God's work. We feasted on fried chicken, mincemeat turnovers, baked beans, toast with apple butter and lemon meringue tarts.

That night as I lay in bed, I thanked God for all the people in my life that loved me, even Grady. With a candle next to my bed giving off some light, I read my Bible until I began to doze off. I was awakened to Mama kissing me on the forehead and blowing out the candle. She put a hand on my forehead and said, "Lord order his steps."

Two weeks after Reverend Zimmerman agreed to train me in the ministry, he and Prof. Sims decided it would be helpful, in my early development, to attend the National Baptist Convention in Philadelphia, Pennsylvania with them. They chose four other young students from Sims High to also attend. Two of them were a grade ahead of me and two others a grade behind. When Poppa agreed to let me go I was elated to no end. For the other students and me, it would be our first trip outside the state of South Carolina.

We left Union early on Thursday morning. Our mothers had prepared apple butter sandwiches and fried chicken for the trip. We were awe-stricken as we traveled north through North Carolina, Virginia and into Washington, D.C. I stared in amazement at the Washington Monument and the Lincoln Memorial. We then drove past the White House and the Capitol building. We left Washington and drove north to Baltimore, Maryland and into Wilmington, Delaware. Being the consummate teacher, Prof. Sims gave us a history lesson pertaining to each major city we passed through on our way to Philadelphia.

When we arrived in Philadelphia late Thursday afternoon, I was mesmerized by the size of the city. We were surrounded by tall buildings, lots of cars, and people scurrying about. We drove through a neighborhood with a lot of white people darker than many Negroes in Union, and with curly hair. Prof. Sims explained to us that in some neighborhoods Negroes and Jews lived next to each other. He told us about integration in the north, but for the most part that subject was frowned upon by the school officials in Union. When I actually saw it, I wondered how long would it take South Carolina to catch up with the rest of the country.

The next two days we attended the conference held in a large convention hall in downtown Philadelphia. I had never before saw that many preachers, most of them immaculately dressed. Prof. Sims seemed to know everyone there. He introduced me to the great Howard Thurman, whose words I have memorized over the years.

Reverend Thurman delivered the keynote address at the convention. I listened intently as he spoke on the importance of social activism, love, justice and forgiveness.

"The Gospel," he said, "can be read as a manual of resistance for the poor and disenfranchised. Jesus is a partner in the pain of suffering and oppression. He suffered at the hands of the Romans. Our pain," his voice rose to a higher crescendo, "can never match the pain of His suffering. But through it all, He found room for forgiveness. That must be our model for the future. We must fight injustice but we must find room to forgive the unjust and you must learn to love your enemy. If you follow Jesus," he concluded, "you must speak out against injustices in the world." Near the very end of his words, he was prophetic. "There are among us," he said. "Leaders who will take up the mantle of Jesus and fight for social and economic justice in this country. One is not complete without the other. Social justice is simply not enough. All people must have the opportunity to the good life, be they Black, white, or any other race."

Reverend Thurman's words would stick with me as I began my study for the ministry under Reverend Zimmerman. After the convention, when we were back in Union, I couldn't wait to get started on my journey.

Reverend Zimmerman's home became my second home. I was over there all the time. I soon became a big brother to his son Matthew, who was seven years old at the time. Matthew would often sit in on our study sessions, and it became quite apparent to me that he would someday make the same commitment to the ministry.

The easiest chore Reverend Zimmerman had was teaching me how to interpret and understand the Bible. It was straightforward and not open for questioning at all. God gave the words in that book to certain men, and they were meant as a road map to salvation. We started with the Old Testament and worked our way through the entire book to include the New Testament. The more difficult job was teaching me how to reconcile my faith in a God that some believed allowed our people to suffer some of the most horrendous abuses in the history of the world. He explained to me, that as a minister, I must be prudent regarding segregation. The most important thing was to make sure that our people were safe. Don't seek out trouble but then, on the other hand, do not allow any man to abuse your manhood.

During the time I studied under Reverend Zimmerman, our families became much closer. Often Grandpa, Poppa and I went fishing on Saturday afternoons with Reverend Zimmerman and Matthew. We drove down to the Broad River, about ten miles outside of Union. We'd park right off the bridge and walk back onto it, climb over the railing and sit on the trestle. With our feet hanging over the edge, we would toss our lines into the river. Often Reverend Zimmerman's attention would not be on catching fish, but making sure his son didn't somehow fall over the edge and down the thirty feet into the water. We stayed there for about four hours, and the conversation always turned to religion, segregation and the future of our people in this country. Even though I was always nervous about possibly falling over the edge, I enjoyed the profound wisdom, and took in what these wise men were saying about our precarious condition living in a country that we viewed as home and we loved, but viewed as second-class citizens to people who did not like us.

Between school assignments and Bible studies, I had very little time for anything else. Latta and I no longer spent as much time together, even though we were still the best of friends. I no longer participated in much of the horseplay during recess or after school. But I still liked the girls, and often made my best friend angry because they always seemed to want to be around me. That was a part of the competitive nature that existed between Latta and me. We competed in everything, but it was always a healthy competition. I did notice, however, that fewer students wanted to hang out with me because I was no longer that jovial, happy go lucky guy I had been before. No more jokes, and especially no more playing the dozens in Mrs. Sims' English class. Whenever we had grammar exercises, with fill in the blanks answers, we filled in the name of another student's mother. That was our way of playing the dozen, but I no longer found making fun of someone's mother a joke.

We always played skin color jokes. I joked about the darker skinned students and they joked about my fair complexion. As my studies increased under Reverend Zimmerman's tutelage, I began to recognize that we all were the same, and that I should not poke fun at someone darker than me. The darker skinned members of our race had always endured the worst punishment from the whites, and I did not want to encourage that as a subject for derision, either against others or against me.

One important point that Reverend Zimmerman constantly stressed in our sessions, was the critical role religion played in the survival of our ancestors during the long and terrible period of slavery. They would often sneak off and hold their own church service, with their version of religion. They dismissed the notion that Christianity was a white man's religion, forced on our ancestors by the slave owners in order to keep them happy and pacified; and also dismissed the idea that the Bible condoned slavery and justified Blacks in the status of slaves. Slaves never believed that whites were their masters, but instead their oppressors much like the Egyptians oppressed the Jews. In those secret church services held in abandoned shacks and under trees covered with old blankets, deep in the woods away from the plantation, and often in the slave cabins late at night, ministers gave a different interpretation of what the new country meant to them.

Whereas Europeans and people from England believed that the new land in America was the promise land, for the Blacks who came over here in the bottom of ships, the new land represented something very different. It was Egypt in the Old Testament. It was a place of misery, pain and suffering. Their homeland in Africa became the promise land, and someday God would part the ocean as He did the Red Sea, and give them safe passage back home. In that sense the captives were similar to the Jews; and therefore were God's chosen people, who had to suffer in order to be saved. That belief in God's salvation through Jesus Christ His son was sufficient to give our ancestors hope for a better life here on earth. Reverend Zimmerman explained that the Emancipation Proclamation and the Thirteenth Amendment to the Constitution were the first step in our total liberation. The second and final step would soon come, and a dedicated follower of Christ would lead it. He admonished me to be prepared to participate in that final phase.

After that particular session with Reverend Zimmerman, my commitment to preach and to God's teachings was complete. I was anxious to get on with my ordination, so I could begin preaching as a minister in the Baptist Church of America. I had to wait for the next general meeting of the PACOLET River Baptist Ministers.

That finally happened during the summer of 1945. Reverend Zimmerman notified me that seven ministers of the association would examine me on Sunday morning and then I would preach my first sermon, assuming I passed the examination. It would all happen at Corinth Baptist Church. It was a blessing that the meeting of ministers was being held at my home church right in Union. That helped create a comfort level for me.

Saturday night before the examination was the most harrowing time of all. I lay in bed tossing and turning, unable to go to sleep. Grady, lying in the bed next to mine, didn't make it any easier for me.

"What you all nervous about?" He asked.

"Why am I nervous?" I scowled. "Because my entire life will be on the line tomorrow morning when I face those seven ministers,"

"Aw, you don't have to worry. You know the Bible inside and out," Grady said.

"What do you know about this stuff?" I shot back at him.

"All you been doing is studying, so you should know it."

"Grady, these are seven ministers who been preaching for years and they really know the Bible," I shrieked.

"So what? You know it too."

"Not as good as they do, and they might try to ask me some trick questions."

"You worry too much," Grady said and turned his back to me.

"And you don't worry enough." I turned to my other side. As I lay there, I tried to take Grady's suggestion and not worry, but the possibility that I might not be ordained stayed on my mind until I finally fell off to sleep.

Next morning I shot straight up in bed, as the sun glared through a crack in the blinds in our bedroom. I made it through the night. Now I just had to make it through the day. The clock on the night stand next to my bed read five-thirty. I needed to get up and review, for probably the hundredth time, notes on my sermon. Grady was still asleep, the house quite still. I pulled myself out of bed and walked across the hall into the bathroom. Last night I laid out my clothes for the day. Poppa had managed to buy me a black suit, white shirt and black tie. He even bought me a new pair of black shoes. I also begged for new underwear. Everything had to be new as I entered a new phase of my life. Poppa smiled when I asked for the underwear and assured me no one would be seeing or concerned with my underwear. But he still bought them for me.

After I finished brushing my teeth, washing my body from head to toe and combing my hair, I hurried back across the hall back into my bedroom. Grady was still snoring. I dressed and left him there, sleeping. It was now a little after six o'clock and Poppa was in the kitchen fixing breakfast.

"Where's Mama?" I asked. It was unusual for her not be in the kitchen preparing breakfast.

"We decided last night that I'd prepare you breakfast before you're ordained and she'd fix a special supper for this evening after you're ordained. Sit down, I got you some bacon, eggs, toast and a little coffee to perk you up."

I sat at the kitchen table while Poppa placed my food in front of me. I felt just like a King. Poppa sat on the other side of table with his plate. We both bowed our heads while he prayed over our breakfast. I was only hours away from becoming an ordained minister but he still took the lead and said the prayer. He was still the father and that's the way it should be, not only now but even after this afternoon's ceremony. He prayed and then we began to eat and talk.

"Son, I got to tell you, we are mighty proud of you," he said as he tossed down a fork full of eggs and followed with a gulp from his coffee cup. "You'll be the first in the family to be a preacher. You're going to start a tradition that I'm sure will be followed in the future. But no matter how many Sanders become preachers you will always be the first."

My chest stuck out a mile. But then I thought what if I don't make it. I'll be the first failure. "You think I'll be approved?" I asked.

"What's more important than what I might think is what you feel in your heart," he said without giving me an answer. "Do you feel God moving inside of you, and do you also feel that He is with you right this minute?"

"Yeah, I guess I really do," I said. At that moment I felt reassured and the spirit of the Lord was filling me with that assurance. "Yes, absolutely I know I have the Lord with me," I continued, now with more confidence.

"James, do you remember when you, Grady and Marionette used to play church, actually hold a funeral and you'd always be the preacher?"

"Yes sir."

"The Lord was sending you a message then. You are meant to

preach the word of the Lord and you are meant to lead his people. This is your calling and there is nothing or no one going to stop you. So just get up there this morning and be a vessel for the Lord." Poppa finished and got up just as Mama walked into the kitchen. She was already dressed.

"Good morning," she said.

"Good morning, Mama."

"Morning," Poppa said. He got up, walked over to the stove and fixed Mama a plate. She sat down next to me.

"Are you ready? She asked.

"Yes ma'am," I said.

"Just what is it you going to preach on this morning?"

I hesitated before answering. I didn't want to reveal my sermon, but this was Mama. "I'm preaching from Matthew, the Fifth Chapter."

"You're doing the Beatitudes," she said.

"Yes, I'm preaching on being blessed. I thought that was perfect since I feel quite blessed having the opportunity to be a disciple of the Lord."

"Listen to you," Mama said. "You're sounding like a preacher already. You know we'll all be sitting there proud as we can be."

"Thank you, Mama. I just hope I don't mess up."

"You won't. Just remember God is in charge and He can never mess up."

Just as she finished, I heard the front door open and knew it was Grandpa. He strolled into the kitchen, dressed and ready to go to church. It was only seven o'clock.

"My grandson about to become a preacher," Grandpa said with a grin spread all over his face. "Come on now we got to get going," he said staring at Poppa. "They going to question James for an hour or so, and we want to be sure to get there early enough so that he can relax."

"Sit down, relax and have a cup of coffee," Poppa said. "We

have plenty of time. His examination begins at nine and we'll leave here at eight-thirty. Is Mama ready?" He asked.

"Yeah, she'll be over here in just a few minutes," Grandpa answered.

This time Mama got up and fixed Grandpa a cup of coffee. "Want any breakfast?" She asked.

"No, I already ate," Grandpa, said. "Just want to get going. James, how you feel and are you ready?"

"Yes sir, I am ready," I answered and thought if one more person asked me if I'm ready, I don't think I will be.

"Where's Grady?" Grandpa asked.

"He's getting up now," Mama said.

"Isn't he going to the service?" Grandpa continued with the questions. "He can't miss his brothers ordination."

"He'll be ready," Daddy chimed back in. "You just drink your coffee and relax. Everything's going to be just fine."

Grandpa finally did relax, drank his coffee, and right at eight-thirty we started out toward Corinth Baptist Church for the most important event in my fifteen years.

Poppa pulled into the parking lot right at eight forty-five. Grandpa had also driven his car and was right behind us. We all walked into the church together. One of the church ushers met us at the door.

"Mr. James Sanders," he said. "You got to come with me. The rest of the family can go on into the sanctuary or downstairs in the basement where they have some light snacks and coffee."

I followed the usher through the sanctuary to a back door, down a narrow hall and into the pastor's study. The only ministers I recognized were Reverend Zimmerman and A.C. Duncan. They both were on the examination team, and I instantly felt more relaxed. I knew they would not let anything happen to me. Besides them, there were five other ministers all sitting around a large conference table. The usher led me up to the front seat. I sat down and waited nervously for this to begin.

Reverend Duncan moderated the questioning. The first and most important question came from him, and that was did I commit my life to teaching the word of God and serving as a disciple of Jesus Christ. After that, the questions came fast and furious and I answered as best I could. At one point I felt that I wouldn't make it, but that is when Reverend Zimmerman smiled as if to say hang in there you will prevail. And prevail I did.

Exactly, one hour after the questioning began and after each pastor had asked me at least two questions, it ended.

"I think you have done quite well," Reverend Duncan said as he brought it to an end. "Now let's get you out to the sanctuary and preach. Then we'll take a vote of the congregation."

"Yes, sir," I said , got up and followed the ministers back into the sanctuary.

The first person I saw sitting in the first row was Grandpa. The rest of the family was sitting two rows behind him. I felt secure seeing my family there to support me. I only wished that Nette could have been there also. But she was away at school. I knew her heart and spirit was there with me.

Once we were seated, Reverend Duncan began the service with a prayer and then invited the choir to sing. Corinth was a praying and singing church, and that is exactly what the choir proceeded to do. That Sunday the mass choir performed. The men, dressed in black suits and white shirts with white ties, and the women all dressed in white with white gloves all stood and lit up the sanctuary with beautiful sounds.

"Your grace and mercy brought me through.

I'm living this moment, because of you.

I want to thank you and praise you too

Your grace and mercy brought me through

Thank you for saving a sinner like me

To tell the world, salvation is free"

The choir had the entire congregation on their feet. They were rocking from side to side. Arms were stretched toward the sky, and were swinging back and forth. An elderly lady shouted,

"Hallelujah, hallelujah, thank you Jesus for your grace and mercy. The more energetic the congregation became the more inspired the choir sang.

"There were times when I just didn't do right,

You watched over me both day and night.

I want to thank you Jesus

I was now so inspired I didn't really need an introduction. When the choir finally sat down I was ready to jump up, rush to the podium and get right into my sermon. God's Holy Spirit was running through me at record speed, and I wanted to get up there and preach His word. But I had to wait for the introduction.

Reverend Duncan got up and strolled up to the podium. He lifted his hands high in the air and said. "If God has blessed you this week, raise your arms to the sky and bless His holy name." With his arms still lifted high he continued, "Welcome Holy Spirit into this place and into my heart. If you love Jesus join in." He paused only for a second or two, and then the entire congregation joined in with their arms raised high. "Welcome Holy Spirit into this place and into my heart."

Reverend Duncan kept this celebration going on for at least five minutes and finally signaled for the congregation to sit down. It was my turn.

"Congregation, we have a young new preacher here with us today. He is asking for you to unanimously confirm him into the ministry of the Lord. I am bringing him up to the podium to bring the word of the Lord to you. Pray for him that he can deliver God's word is such a way that you all will feel confident in confirming him into the ministry. Let's bring James Sanders to us with a welcome." He finished, turned and walked back to his seat.

I rose and strolled to the pulpit. I said a silent prayer for strength and God's deliverance, as I began my ministry with a joyous song.

"When we all get to heaven,

What a day of rejoicing that will be"

When we all see Jesus

We'll sing and shout the victory."

I knew the congregation was with me as they stood and sang along. After five minutes they were fired up and I was ready to preach. I motioned for them to take their seats, and then began my first and most important sermon. It was amazing how fast the time passed by. I wasn't aware that I was the one preaching, as the Holy Spirit took over for the next half hour and words flowed from me to the congregation with ease. I now knew I could do this with the help of God. I was willing to be that vessel to deliver His word and after the sermon was over I felt better than I'd ever felt in my entire life.

Once I sat back down, Reverend Duncan called for the vote from the congregation. It was a resounding "yes." I was now an ordained minister of the Baptist faith. The feeling was exhilarating. When Reverend Duncan finally brought the service to an end, I stood at the front entrance-way to the church and shook hands for the next half hour.

When it was over, we returned home and Mama again fixed an excellent meal. The family laughed and I celebrated with the ones I loved, my acceptance into the ministry to preach the word of the one I loved most, Jesus Christ, my Lord and Savior.

5

My senior year at Sims High School was extremely productive as I continued to mature. My grades were outstanding, straight A's, and my knowledge of the Bible was steadily improving. Because of my academic accomplishments and my leadership skills among the other students, Prof. Sims chose me as Valedictorian speaker for our high school graduation ceremony.

As the graduation day neared, I thought about the amount of knowledge I had attained from so many incredibly intelligent men. I wondered could life become any more exciting than what the past five years at Sims High School had been. I began to give a great deal of thought about where I wanted to continue my education. I decided to follow in Reverend Zimmerman's shoes and attend Benedict College near Columbia, South Carolina. It was the premiere Black college in the state, and had a superb track record for turning out outstanding men who went on to accomplish many great things in their fields of endeavor.

I knew for sure that I would major in religion and a minor in English. Even though my goal was to someday make ministry a full time Profession, that was not realistic in South Carolina. Most ministers had to start out at very small churches that did not have a budget large enough to afford their minister a salary. Reverend Zimmerman had a large enough church so that he didn't have to work another job; he was still the principal at a small school that actually went from Kindergarten through twelfth grade. Prof. Sims was also pastor of Limestone Missionary Baptist Church in Gaffney but his primary means of income was from teaching school.

In Union, there was a very thin line between teacher and preacher. The teachers who were not ministers were required to dedicate much of their spare time to work within the church. The community leaders and townspeople insisted that those in charge of educating the young must not only be dedicated to education, but also totally committed to Jesus Christ. It only made sense that if I planned to preach, I must also know how to teach the very same children, who would someday become leaders in the church

On graduation day I was a nervous wreck simply because I knew I had to speak on behalf of the entire graduating class. The very week after Prof. Sims informed me that I would deliver the speech I went to work to get the right words on paper. Prof. Sims, Grandpa, Poppa and Reverend Zimmerman helped me structure my words so they made sense, had real meaning, and most important were coherent. I practiced my delivery in front of a mirror, in front of Grady, Mama, Poppa, and Grandpa. But I refused to let Latta listen. I didn't want anyone from the graduating class to know what I would say prior to the ceremony.

At two o'clock on a Saturday in June 1947, the ninety graduating students marched into the school auditorium and lined up behind the podium on the stage. The auditorium was packed with proud parents, city officials, and interested men and women from the community. The South Carolina flag was placed at one end of the stage and the United States flag at the other end. Prof. Sims and Reverend Zimmerman, who would open the graduation proceedings with a prayer, sat in two large chairs in front of us. The mayor, superintendant of schools and president of the Union School Board sat in the front row. As I looked out at them, I couldn't help but wonder would they be there if they knew some of the things Prof. Sims and our other teachers often said about them, behind the closed doors in the classroom. I also wondered would they approve of my comments on behalf of the graduating class.

I planned to tell the audience that the 1947 graduates of Sims High School planned to make a difference in this country. We would no longer sit idly by and allow our people to be treated as second-class citizens, because we know we are as much citizens of this country as any other race. I also planned to tell my fellow graduates that our education had just begun, and it is imperative that we get college training that would prepare us to assume the responsibility to make the lives of our people much more bearable. Despite warnings from a few of my fellow students, I had to sneak in a few words on how tragic it was for a country to allow its enemies to eat where its citizens couldn't.

Before marching into the auditorium, a young boy warned me about the trouble I could cause by crossing the invisible line that dictated what Black people could say in the presence of white folks. He infuriated me, and I told him that we must take a stand against the insults and attacks we had suffered over the years. We had to let them know we did not appreciate having to walk to school while the white students rode, and then had the nerve to throw objects at us out of the school bus window. We did not expect our children to have to endure that kind of treatment. Sometimes we were our own worst enemy. We allowed those people to mistreat us because we couldn't afford to get involved. But the real truth was that we couldn't afford not to get involved. In the final portion of my speech, I would tell everyone that this is our America, this is our South Carolina and our Union, and that in the very near future we must claim ownership. There would be a battle but we had to be the victors because right and God were on our side.

I glared out at the audience and noticed a slight smile cross Poppa's face, as I delivered my speech. The city officials did not smile, and their faces seemed to turn red. It didn't matter because I was in charge, and this was my platform to tell them and the rest of the city that this graduating class represented the best that America had to offer. We were Dr. Du Bois' talented tenth and were determined to carry out his mandate. I couldn't see Prof. Sims' face because he sat behind me, but I could just imagine the joy he felt. I was demonstrating the power of his teaching and the influence he had over us for the past five years. "Give them to me and they will never have to plow a cotton field or pick cotton," was his promise to all our parents, and it was the real theme behind my speech. My final words were directed at this great man. I turned and looked directly at him.

"You sir, have brought us this far and we thank you for the job you have done. You made each of us raise our sights to a higher plateau and convinced us to believe that we could achieve what we put our minds on doing. Now we are prepared to take it from here.

All ninety students promise to fulfill your wishes to make this a better world for our people, and to make Union, South Carolina a place known for the talent it has produced within our race. We say thank you and may God bless you for what you have done."

With those final words, the entire graduating class clapped loudly in deference to him. Our gesture was contagious because the audience also stood and clapped in honor of him. I noticed, however, that the white officials did not get up. They faintly brought their hands together, as not to appear too obnoxious by not giving this man the honor he deserved.

When all the dignitaries had spoken, Prof. Sims then called each one of the graduates to the podium and handed them their degree. As I approached a broad smile crossed his face.

"Great job," he whispered and handed me the diploma.

I smiled and returned to my place among the students. Finally, when every student had been recognized, we threw our caps in the air as an indication that it was all over, and we were high school graduates.

"We don't have money to help you go to Benedict," Poppa said as the family sat in the living room conducting one of our family meetings, the night after my graduation. This time the discussion was about me and my college plans. "You know we have to help your sister finish her college, and we just don't have money to help both of you," he continued.

"I know," I said rather subdued.

"Then how do you plan to pay tuition?" Mama asked.

"Reverend Zimmerman promised that the church would help out when it could, and I'm going to work the summer at Chalk's."

"Benedict is a Baptist college and you are a Baptist preacher," Poppa said. "Why don't you contact the school and see if they might have something you can do to pay toward your tuition."

"Do you think Grandpa would call down there and set up a meeting for me with the right people?" I asked. "Everybody in the entire state knows Grandpa, and they respect him. All I need is a meeting and I'll do the rest."

"I'll have him do it tomorrow. But if he gets it done for you then you have to make sure you don't let him down," Poppa added.

"I'll be doing what I love to do, that is increasing my knowledge of the Bible and getting my Bachelors Degree so I can teach as well as preach. There is no way I can let him down, because if I did, I'd be letting myself and most important God down," I said with a bit of confidence and a tinge of defiance. How dare Poppa have any doubts that I might not succeed. Failure was not in my vocabulary. After five years under Prof. Sims there was no way I could even imagine not succeeding.

Poppa glared at me with irritation all over his face. I never meant to be disrespectful to him but I had to make it very clear that not only would I attend Benedict but would reach the top echelon of success. I was ready to become a leader of my race in South Carolina. I only needed for Grandpa to make that call.

It took two weeks for Grandpa to get that meeting. In fact, it was really Reverend Zimmerman who finally intervened and convinced Dr. John A. Bacoats, the President of Benedict to meet with me. Dr. Bacoats was a Baptist preacher and had been the pastor at one of the largest African American churches in Baton Rogue, Louisiana before becoming president of a number of colleges. He had taken over at Benedict after Dr. John Jacob Starks, the college's first African American president, retired in 1945. Reverend Zimmerman had met Dr. Bacoats at a national Baptist convention prior to him coming to Benedict. That opened the door for their conversation. When he told the president that I was an up and coming Baptist preacher who received his calling at 15 years of age, and had studied under him for the past two years, he was more than willing to talk about how the college might be able to help me with my tuition.

Poppa and I left Union early on the Monday, two days after the Fourth of July which fell on a Saturday. Even though I had been driving for a couple years and had my driver's license, Poppa insisted on driving all the way to Columbia where the college is located. We arrived at the school just before noon. Our appointment was for one o'clock so we had over an hour to wait. We decided to eat lunch at A and B Soul Food House. It was one of the best-known Negro restaurants in South Carolina, having been around since 1912. There was no doubt in my mind that I would have many meals there, whenever I could afford it.

A and B was located directly across from the campus on Hardin Street. We entered the restaurant and sat at a table with a window view of the campus. Benedict was located on a 110 acre old plantation. Massive oak trees spread their limbs over the campus and one road led to Convention Hall. We were looking directly at it. A tall, slim waitress approached our table and handed us menus.

"What y'all want to eat this afternoon," she said.

"Give me the fried chicken, mashed potatoes and okra with corn bread," Poppa said. "What you want James?"

I stared at the menu. It all sounded so good I didn't know what to choose. Finally I said.

"Hamburger with fries and a soda."

"Be right back with y'all's order," the waitress said, then turned and walked away.

Momentarily, Poppa and I stared out the window across the street at the large oak tree that seemed to be protecting the campus from the bright and hot sun.

"Hundreds of your ancestors found shade under that very tree that now covers the campus," Poppa said.

"You think so," I said.

"Definitely. Where they once stood in bondage you will be standing as a college student. That is some progress, not enough but a start."

"Why didn't you go to college?" I asked.

"Couldn't, cause we were too poor. Your granddaddy did the best he could but we were only a few years removed from slavery. And you have to know that our people were freed but not given any security, no money or land. The government had promised to give all freed slaves forty acres and a mule so they could work their land, but that never happened. All the land was given back to the very people who caused the war, the plantation owners." He paused as if to get his thoughts together. "While we were driving up here did you notice all those folks out in the fields working?"

"Yes."

"They're sharecroppers and been sharecroppers for decades since the Emancipation. Instead of giving them land they could own, they were forced back on the plantation to work for the very people who claimed they owned them before the war. They'll probably stay in that condition for generations because they feel no hope for the future. That's why many of them drink and get drunk to escape their feeling of hopelessness."

"How did Granddaddy manage to escape the plantation?" I was asking questions I had thought about for years; it seemed the appropriate time and setting to express my curiosity.

"Despite how poor we were, he refused to let them deny his manhood. He refused to spend one day on a plantation because it was such a terrible reminder of our past. He took up a trade and moved to Union."

"That's why you also became a painter?"

"Yes, I followed him in his trade. It was honest work and we didn't make a lot of money, but at least we could hold our heads high and know that we were our own men, and didn't belong to nobody. Many of the people on those plantations working as sharecroppers in many ways still belong to the owners. They can't leave because they are in so much debt to the white folks. It is what you can call the 1940's version of slavery."

"I guess that's why Prof. Sims says give him the children and after six months they'll never go back to plowing."

"That's right and that's why it's so important that young men like Latta and you get your education, so you can make the same promise to mothers and fathers in the years to come."

I listened to Poppa and understood what he was trying to get across to me. But my future was not in the classroom like Prof. Sims, but in the church like Reverend Zimmerman. Latta and I had committed to the ministry, but knew the chances of getting a church that could support us right away were very slim. We also knew the professions opened for young Blacks in 1947 South Carolina was either primary or secondary teaching. I would pursue a degree in teaching, but many of my classes would be in the field of religious studies. I recognized that I could serve my people best in the ministry.

"You understand what I'm telling you, James?"

Poppa snapped me out of my musing.

"Yes sir, I do."

The waitress approached our table with a tray of sizzling food hot out of the kitchen.

"Good, now let's eat and then go talk with Dr. Bacoates."

Poppa and I sat in the two chairs in front of Dr. Bacoates desk. He leaned forward across the desk and looked over the top of his eyeglasses. Poppa began the conversation.

"Thank you for agreeing to meet with us on such short notice," he said.

"My pleasure," Dr. Bacoates said and then looked directly at me. "I understand we have a new young preacher in this young man," he continued. He finished, then turned and glared over at Poppa.

"He got his calling when he was fifteen and has trained under Reverend Zimmerman," Poppa said.

"Yes, that's what I was told by Reverend Zimmerman when he called about the young man attending Benedict College. If he trained with my friend then I know he has learned two important and valuable lessons. The first being that he must totally understand the Bible from the beginning to the end in order to spread the word of God, and to teach the Gospel of Jesus Christ. The second being that he must reach out to his people and help save them from all the evils and the temptations they confront every day."

I sat and listened just like I was not in the room. I knew at some point they would get around to the subject at hand, and the reason we were there. My anxiety level was building. I wanted to get to the point and know if I would get help from the school. My going to Benedict all hinged on what Dr. Bacoates could offer me.

"James is a good boy with a great foundation, having attended Sims High School for the past five years."

"Ah, yes Dr. Sims," Dr. Bacoates said with a smile. "Now that is a good man and a brilliant individual. He's very knowledgeable on the Classics and on history. Students coming out of his high school are well prepared for the rigors of college life."

"The Negro community of Union is fortunate to have a man of his caliber teaching their children," Poppa said. "He tells every parent that you give your son to him for six months then he will never plow a cotton field again in life."

"And that's what it is all about, because our people have plowed enough cotton fields to last the next two hundred years." Dr. Bacoates reared back in his chair and pushed his eyeglasses back up on his nose. "I believe I have work for this young man to help defray the cost of his tuition."

My attention perked up and I slid up in my chair. Finally, they got around to the subject I wanted to hear discussed.

"He has enough money to cover his tuition. The church raised most of that money, and then he has saved the money he's gotten over the years for preaching at different churches and at ceremonies," Poppa said. "We only need his room and board to be covered. And he won't be a drain on you on weekends, because he's going to come home every weekend."

"Let me stress the job I'm going to assign him requires that he be here early Monday morning so he needs to make sure he gets back here Sunday evening. We have a number of young ministers who are full time students. They leave campus on Friday and don't return sometimes until Monday because they have church service on Sunday evening. Some of them live as far away as Charleston. Dr. Riley who is Dean of Men, usually schedules most of their classes for Tuesdays and the rest of the week. James will probably have the same schedule, since he will be living in the dorm with the other students who are ministers. But he will not have the luxury of getting back here on Monday. He has to be here by five o'clock in the morning on Monday."

"That'll be no problem, Poppa said.

I adjusted my body in the chair from one side to the other. My heart raced as my anxiety continued to build. I wanted to know exactly what I would be doing that required me to be back on campus late Sunday.

"Good," Dr. Bacoates said. He then got up and started around his desk. "Then let me show you what he'll be doing."

We followed him out of his office and the building. As we walked across the campus he gave us somewhat of a tour calling out the names of the different buildings.

"That building in front of you is Lodge Hall. That's where a number of classrooms are located. James will probably be taking some classes in there, especially those dealing with religious studies. We have three outstanding scholars who teach the classes. Dr. C. H. Brown who is the Dean of the Dr. J. J. Starks School of Theology teaches Theology and Homiletics, Dr. L. C. Jenkins teaches Old Testament and Dr. Maxie S. Gordon teaches New Testament and Religious Education. They are all located in that building." He pointed at a building next to Lodge Hall. "That building there is the men's dormitory for students who are pastors." Beyond was another building he pointed to.

"That's Osborne Hall. It's the girl's dormitory. Definitely off limits to the men." He chuckled.

Dr. Bacoates took us inside the gymnasium and introduced us to the coach and a few of the basketball players. The coach had just blown his whistle indicating that is was time for a break.

A young boy bounced the basketball over toward us. "Hey, my name is Taft Watson. I'm from Marion County, anytime you want to shoot hoops, look me up."

I smiled. "I might just take you up on that offer."

"You see James, here at Benedict we are a family," Dr. Bacoates said, "and we take care of one another."

I felt so proud that I'd be attending Benedict. We left the gymnasium for the rest of the tour.

We finally walked up the steps of an old wooden two-story building. Once inside we went down a flight a stairs into a basement area. The room was filled with long tables and chairs. Up front was a serving area and beyond was a large wrought iron stove. Dr. Bacoates walked to the front and stopped in front of the stove. He opened the bottom. It was filled with ashes.

"Your job, young man, will be to empty these ashes early in the morning and light the fire to heat the stove. The students eat their meals in here and everything is prepared on this stove. So you see it is absolutely necessary that you be here and have the fire going by five thirty in the morning. Breakfast starts at seven and if the stove isn't lit, the cooks cannot prepare the food and you will have a whole lot of angry students, and of course me also. Reverend Bates, who isn't here today, is in charge of the cafeteria and you will be working for him." He paused and closed the door to the opening in the bottom. "For this you will receive free room and board. Is this something you feel you can do?"

"Don't worry, Dr. Bacoates, he can do it," Daddy said.

"No sir," Dr. Bacoates shot back. "I need to hear James commit to this assignment. With all due respects, Mr. Sanders, you will not be here. It will be your son and I must hear from him that he will be committed to doing this work. If he does then he has the job and therefore his room and board."

Both men looked directly at me.

"Yes sir, no doubt I can and will do it."

"Will you make sure you are back here Sunday evenings so you can take care of your responsibilities by five thirty in the morning?"

"Yes sir, I will make sure I am back here on time."

Dr. Bacoates held his hand out to me.

"Congratulations, welcome to Benedict College."

I nervously shook his hand.

"Thank you sir," I said.

Dr. Bacoates turned to Poppa. "Please have him back here the Sunday before registration. Dr. Riley will take care of him from that point forward."

"We will definitely have him here." Poppa said.

We walked back up the stairs and out into the bright afternoon sun. Dr. Bacoates walked with us to the car.

"Drive safely and we will see you in a couple months James."

"Thank you sir," I said, got in the car and Poppa and I started back to Union. I was now a college student and was entering an important new phase of my life.

6.

"I won't be attending Benedict with you," Latta said as we sat on the porch at his parent's house, drinking homemade lemonade.

"What you talking about," I said. "You have to go to college. Prof. Sims would practically have a stroke if he knew you weren't going to college. You were one of the best students in our graduating class."

"I'm definitely going to college," Latta said. "But we can't afford the tuition or the room and board, so I'm going to go to Rock Hill Community College. I got relatives that live there and I can stay with them for two years."

Much of the joy I felt about getting into Benedict dissipated as I now had to face the prospect of going there without my best friend. I felt devastated.

"It won't be the same without you. We been together since 1943, and now you going somewhere else."

"It's not that I don't want to, but you have to understand that we came here from the country. My Daddy was a farmer on somebody else's land. We aren't fortunate like you. Your folks own their own home and got a good income. I'm happy for you but I just don't have it that good."

"You going to come to Benedict after community college?" I asked, not knowing what else to say after what he had just said. I felt somewhat embarrassed. I didn't want us to be better than any other family, especially my best friend Latta's family. Most important to me was that I would miss his competition. We always competed against each other, and that kind of competitiveness made us both better students. Now I wouldn't have that and it would be different. But what else could I say.

"Yeah, I plan to come on over to Benedict. It's the very best training ground for future ministers and it's Baptist. Where else could I go? Not Allen Methodist across the street from Benedict."

We both laughed.

"You got a point there," I added. "The Baptist religion is the cornerstone of our race and actually the very foundation."

"James, you going to be just fine. You're smart, aggressive and everyone on that campus is going to like you, especially the girls."

'The girls are attracted to me, aren't they?" I said and smiled.

"There you go with that ego. You'd better put it in check before it gets you in trouble. I understand Dr. Bacoates is old school and very conservative. He don't tolerate too much messing around at Benedict."

"I know."

"You're going there to get an education, not a wife."

"But a wife someday has to be a part of both of our lives. You can't be a minister for long without a wife. Folks here won't stand for no single, playboy minister in these parts. That might be accepted up north where the morals are pretty shot. But not down here."

"Don't worry, the right woman will come along and you'll know she's right, cause God will let you know."

I stood up on the steps where we'd been sitting in the hot sun for the past half hour.

"In the meantime, I got to get over to the church. Dr. Zimmerman wants me to preach on Sunday and wants to check out my sermon."

"You moving up in the world," Latta said with a smile. "Preaching at the most prestigious and one of the biggest churches in Union. Boy, you're on your way."

I patted my friend on the back. "No, we both are on our way," I said in a bittersweet tone. I would truly miss Latta.

"See you later." He smiled and waved as he walked back into the house.

"You got it," I said, turned and headed toward Corinth.

As I strolled into Corinth, the first person I saw was Malachi Duncan standing near the entrance to Dr. Zimmerman's office talking with him. What a surprise. I didn't know he'd gotten back to Union even though the war had been over for two years. He looked just as I remembered him before he left.

He stared over at me and smiled.

"James Sanders, how you doing, young man?" He said as we hugged.

"I'm blessed," I said. "When did you get back?"

"Been back in Union for a couple days."

"Where you been all this time? The war ended two years ago."

"I spent some time up in New York with relatives. But I didn't like it at all. Nothing like home."

"What else you been doing?" We both were being rather rude. Dr. Zimmerman stood there listening to the two of us. We carried on just like he wasn't there.

"Well, I got married and now I have two kids. I have a family."

"Congratulations," I said. "What do you plan to do?"

"I'm enrolling in Benedict College, and of course I'm going to be a minister."

My excitement grew. I was losing one friend but now another friend from home would be going to Benedict with me.

"I was just telling Reverend Zimmerman that the government has this thing called the G.I. Bill passed by Congress. It pays veterans to go to school."

"You mean they're going to let Negroes take advantage of it also?" I asked.

"They can't stop us. We went over there and fought for this country just like the white man. It would be super-hypocritical of them to try to exclude Negro veterans. I know you all heard about the Tuskegee Airmen, and how well they flew their planes protecting the bombers from German planes attacking them. Then there were Black units who fought with General Patton in Italy and the Black tanker brigade. General Patton had nothing but praise for our fighting ability. So yes, I'm going to have Uncle Sam pay for me to go to college."

Malachi's praise of our fighting men took me back to the time we discussed in class the fact that German soldiers could eat in restaurants in Union that would only serve us from a side window, outside the building. The German fighter pilots who were trying to shoot our planes from the air could, if captured, eat at places where the men who prevented them from killing Americans, couldn't.

"Hey young men," Reverend Zimmerman finally spoke up. "Why don't you all come on in my office and you can continue talking."

"Sorry Reverend Zimmerman," I said. "But we haven't seen each other since Malachi left Union five years ago. We got a lot of catching up to do."

"Well do it in my office. I have a few errands to run. So why don't you all talk and when I get back, James, we can get started."

Malachi and I sauntered into Reverend Zimmerman's office and sat in the two chairs in front of his desk. The pastor went in the other direction.

"Is your family going to move down to Columbia?" I asked.

"No, they're going to stay here in Union. I'm going to commute back and forth. I'll go down to Benedict on Sunday evening and come back here on Friday."

"Are you serious?" I asked as the excitement in me continued to build. "How you going to get back and forth?"

A broad smile spread across Malachi's face.

"Well, I bought myself a 1941 Pontiac when I got out of the service. So I'll be driving back and forth."

I lifted my head toward the ceiling and whispered. "Thank you God. You are truly wonderful and great."

"What you say?" Malachi asked.

"Just a small prayer to God for His magnificent blessings," I said. "I have a situation that you might be able to help me out with."

"What's that?"

"I got this job at Benedict that covers my room and board. But it calls for me being on campus at five thirty Monday through Friday. The problem is that I'll be preaching on Sundays in some of the local churches."

"Congratulations," Malachi said. "My father told me he ordained you into the ministry."

"Thank you," I said. "But you see, my ministry will make it very difficult to do my job unless I can get back to Benedict by late Sunday evening." I slid up to the tip of the chair and leaned toward Malachi. "God sent you to me as an answer to my prayer. If you're going to be coming home on Friday and then going back on Sunday, I can ride with you. Of course I'll be willing to pay you something."

"Absolutely," Malachi said. "I can use the company and I'll have someone to talk to you when I get sleepy. That's an hour and a half ride through some very boring country."

"We have a deal," I said and stuck out my hand.

We shook.

"You got it. For the next four years we're going to be company for each other. Sounds like a plan."

Just as we finished Reverend Zimmerman walked back into the office.

"From the looks on the two of your faces, looks like you worked something out," he said.

"We sure did," Malachi said. "We're going to be riding partners for the next four years."

"And just think of how much you all can talk about regarding the ministry, your future churches and your future leadership. Sounds good to me." A smile spread across Reverend Zimmerman's face.

"Do you mind if I sit in while you discuss James' preaching this Sunday?" Malachi asked

"Not if James doesn't mind."

"No, I don't mind," I said. "We're going to be sitting in on each other for many years in the future. Might as well start now."

Let's get started then," Reverend Zimmerman said as he sat at his desk. "James, I understand you're going to preach from John 3:16," he continued. "Let me hear what you plan to tell the congregation."

That Sunday morning was extremely hot in Union. We had been going through a hot spell for a couple of weeks. So as I took my chair near the pulpit next to Reverend Zimmerman little beads of sweat ran down my face. Before leaving the house that morning, Mama had given me one of Poppa's handkerchiefs. She told me to keep it in my front suit pocket so it would be easy to get to when I started preaching and sweating.

Large electric fans were placed at each end of the sanctuary but they seemed to be causing nothing but hot air to swirl around. Two of the ushers turned the fans backward to draw out some of the heat. Men in suits and women in colorful dresses and large hats sat fanning themselves with fans provided by Foster Funeral Home. This Sunday's service was dedicated to the youth, as was every third Sunday in the month. I had already preached two youth day services at Corinth, but each time I was just as nervous as the first one.

I watched as the youth choir marched down the center aisle and up to the uplifted platform behind where we sat. Many of my friends were ushering people to the very few seats still available. Momentarily I thought how wise for Reverend Zimmerman to allow us to run the service because some day we would be the heart beat of the church. He was preparing us well for that day.

The service began with a prayer delivered by Matthew Zimmerman, and then the welcome to visitors was done by Grady.

It was the first time he'd actually participated in the service. It dawned on me that I hadn't spent as much time with my baby brother as I should, due to the many events and circumstances surrounding my life. I made a mental note to spend an evening with just him, before I left for Benedict.

As the ushers passed the collection plate for the tithes and offerings, I glared down at the first row where Poppa and Grandpa sat. I knew they were proud of me. Sitting right behind them in the second row was Mama and Grandma. They were equally as proud. It was every mother's dream that her son would commit his life to Christ and take up the ministry. I had made that commitment and Mama sat there proud as any mother could possibly be for her son. Next to Mama, were my two closest friends, Latta and Malachi. Either one of them could be sitting where I was and deliver just as dynamic a sermon. But they both had just begun their ministries, and still had to be ordained. Nette sat in the second row with our cousin Ruby Smith. Grady sat in the back with some of the other younger boys.

The kind of joy that makes you want to cry took over my body momentarily. I thought how fortunate I was to have my entire family there to support me, and how fortunate I was to be the first Sanders man to accept ministry as his calling. I knew in the future there would be many Sanders to follow me and become men who dedicated their lives to preaching the word of the Lord and our Savior Jesus Christ. I had to be good and serve as a great role model for those who would follow me into the pulpit.

Finally, it was time. Reverend Zimmerman approached the pulpit and addressed the congregation.

"Once again, I have the pleasure to bring to the pulpit a young, dynamic preacher who is home grown right here at Corinth. And I am proud to tell you all that he is now a college student. He has been admitted to Benedict College, a good Baptist College and one that I also attended."

The entire congregation jumped to their feet and began to applaud. It was a thunderous sound that resonated throughout the sanctuary.

Reverend Zimmerman waited for the men and women to sit back down and continued. "Benedict has a reputation of turning out some of the most powerful preachers in South Carolina. And this young man will be no different. So right after our youth choir delivers a song, the next voice you will hear will be that of young James W. Sanders." Reverend Zimmerman returned to his seat and smiled at me just before he sat down.

The choir began and their voices were as radiant and beautiful as if they were angels singing down on us from Heaven.

"If anybody ask me where I am going," they began. *"I'm going up to yonder, I'm going up to yonder to be with my Lord. If anybody ask me where I am going."* Their voices rose to a very high crescendo. *"I'm going up to yonder to be with my Lord."*

I turned and looked back at young students who had or were still attending Sims High School, bringing such sounds into the sanctuary. I could feel my blood rising up to my brain and excitement invaded my very being. Momentarily, I felt choked up as the choir continued to set a mood with song that I wasn't sure I could match with words. They finished on a very high note, and I slowly rose from my chair and strolled to the pulpit.

"Please stand for the reading of John 3:16." I waited for the congregation to find the passage in their Bibles. "I tell you the truth," I began to quote from Jesus to His disciples. "No one can see the Kingdom of God unless he is born again." I stopped right there as Reverend Zimmerman had instructed me to do. "You may be seated," I said to the congregation.

Another lesson I learned from Reverend Zimmerman as well as Reverend A.C. Duncan was to always be in control of your congregation when you were preaching. As an eighteen-year-old boy turned preacher I did just that, and for the next half hour I delivered one of my most effective messages to date. God took over and I knew the Holy Spirit sent the words through me to His people. I followed like an obedient servant.

It was my beginning and I felt good about all the wonderful things happening in my life.

7.

Highway 215 was a two-lane road that traversed a lot of countryside from Union to Columbia and right to Benedict College. That would be the road Malachi and I would drive twice a week for the next four years. As we started out for the first time in the fall of 1947, I suffered from anxiety. Despite all the encouragement a person could need from family and friends, and despite my confidence in my ability, there was still that feeling of apprehension as to whether I could make it in the college setting. I would be competing with young men from all over the state of South Carolina and even a few from other parts of the south. My training at Sims High School was as good as it gets and probably better than at most schools. But still there was that small burning doubt about my ability. I am sure Malachi felt the same, even though he had much more worldly experience than me.

He picked me up at five in the morning. The dew on the grass in the front yard for some odd reason glistened that day. Mama had stayed up all night cooking for Malachi and me. We had enough sandwiches to last, even after we arrived at college. As we congregated at the front door for our good byes, I felt an ache deep inside. I was leaving my comfort level. The living room where Nette, Grady and I had played church, the room where Grady and I wrestled, and where the voice of Nette resonated, "James and Grady, you'd best do your chores before we all get into trouble," would become a memory.

Mama hugged me so tightly at the door I thought I'd lose my breath. Poppa shook my hand. Grady and I hugged.

"I love you big brother," he said.

"Not as much as I love you, little brother," I said.

As we rode down the highway, a wave of emotions overtook me; a combination of sadness, excitement, hope and fear all rolled up together. It wasn't long before we were riding in country staring at rows and rows of cotton fields. We passed the Woodland Plantation right outside Carlisle. Then we passed through Whitmire, Newberry, and every little town in between.

Sharecroppers were already in the fields. Every once in a while they would look up from their bent over positions and glare at the two Negro boys driving in a relatively new Pontiac. As I glared back at them, I wondered what must be going through their minds. We had driven for about a half hour before I finally broke the silence.

"Are you ready for this?" I asked.

"For what?"

"You know, college life, the ministry and the responsibility that goes with all of that."

"I don't think we have a choice." Malachi momentarily took his eyes off the road and glared over at me. "I don't think we're privileged, but blessed. With God's blessings goes a greater commitment to help His people."

"I love the verse, 'what you do to the least of mine you do to me.' And look what white people have done to our people all these years." I paused and looked out the window. "I mean, just look around you. Look at our people. Up at the break of day and work late into the night. And for what? A mere pittance."

"I know cause I been there and did that," Malachi replied. "Sharecropping's got to be the worst job in the entire country. It's hard work, with very little pay and no other rewards. Negroes in the fields just live from day to day. They survive, they don't dream."

"I know one thing for sure," I said with my voice rising. "When I get my church, I'm going to teach my people how to live a life that assures them a place in God's kingdom, but I'm also going to teach them how to make it in this world. I don't believe God wants his preachers to forget about the suffering here on earth."

"But never forget your first obligation is to save souls for Jesus." Again Malachi took his eyes off the road to look directly at me.

"I know that, but I still believe we can do both. Don't you want to help the people who believe in you as a preacher to live a better life right here on earth." I grabbed a couple pieces of chicken out of the bag and gave Malachi a piece.

"Absolutely," Malachi shot back at me as he took a bite of the drumstick.

"It will be our generation of preachers who will take on the evils of this country and change things." I also took a bite of a drumstick.

"Yeah, and there are a whole lot of evils. God's going to punish these people someday for the way they have treated the Negro for centuries."

It was a little past ten o'clock in the morning when we drove up Hardin Street toward the main campus. The street was alive with students hurrying to the administration building. I stared out the window in wonderment at Morgan Hall, Pratt Hall, Duckett Hall, all located down campus row. Malachi slowed down as we passed Antisel Chapel. We would spend a lot of time in that building. As we drove past A and B restaurant I thought about how good the food was when Poppa and I ate there. I knew that would be my place to eat, whenever I had a little extra money. Malachi finally pulled onto the campus and found a parking spot for students.

"This is it," he said as he turned the car off.

"I'm ready," I said. "I'm ready for it to begin and ready for it to end so that I can get to my ministry."

"Be patient, young man," Malachi said. We both got out of the car and headed toward the administration building. "Remember, patience is a virtue and every good preacher must have a lot of it."

After standing in line for over an hour, Malachi and I got our class assignments as well as our living quarters. To my disappointment, Dr. Riley told me that I would not be taking any religious classes my first two years. I had to take the basic lower division requirements that included Science, English, French,

Sociology and Negro History.

To my dismay and also extreme disappointment, Malachi and I were assigned separate dorms. He was assigned to the dorm for war veterans, and I was with the other ministers and ministerial students. The only consolation was that we had two classes together, Sociology and Negro History. Once we finished registering, Malachi took off to his new living quarters, and I headed down to the cafeteria to report to duty with Reverend Bates.

"If you place the wood in here so it can breathe, you going to get a mighty fine fire," Reverend Bates explained as I stood right behind him and watched as he demonstrated the best way to get a good fire going in the morning. We were the only two in the cafeteria and I could hear an echo every time he talked. "Now it's going to take about a half hour to really get the stove hot enough to cook on, so you got to get down here on time," he continued. "The cooks will be right in here at six, so you know what that means."

"Yes sir," I said.

"What does it mean?"

"That I have to be here by five thirty."

"You remember that and we won't have any problems at all." Reverend Bates stood up and closed the door to the stove. "This campus is already full of new and returning students so they're going to be packing this place real early. You can eat after you get the fire going. You have any questions?"

"No sir."

"Then good, you'd better get over to your dorm and find out where you going to be sleeping. I'll see you in the morning."

"You're going to be here at five thirty?" I asked

"Absolutely. I'll be here until I know I can trust you. I don't want nothing going wrong."

"Reverend Bates, I need this job to pay my tuition. There is no way I'm not going to be here unless I am deathly sick."

"I hear you and I believe you, but I'll still see you in the morning."

"Thank you, sir," I said and then hurried out of the cafeteria, up the steps and out of the building.

As I strolled into my room on the second floor of the men's dorm, my roommate had already staked out his claim. He was sprawled out on his bed reading from the Bible. He looked up to greet me.

"Welcome," he said. "I was wondering if you were ever going to get here." He got up and sauntered over to where I stood and extended his hand. "I'm Walter Jackson from Charleston, South Carolina.

I shook his hand and said, "James William Sanders from Union, South Carolina."

Walter strolled back over to his bed and sprawled out across it. "Hope you don't mind that I grabbed this side of the room."

"Don't matter to me," I said. "Bed is a bed. And you'll probably be here more than me, since I'll be going home every weekend."

He sat up in the bed. "You're going back to Union every weekend?" He repeated my words just as if he didn't believe me.

"Yeah, I do a lot of preaching around there and out in the country."

"You're ordained already?"

"Yeah, I been ordained now for two years."

Walter sat on the side of the bed. "How old were you when got your calling?" He asked.

"Fifteen," I proudly replied.

"You been preaching since you was fifteen, that's wonderful. I'm working on my ordination right now. But I won't be going back home every weekend."

"My friend's going to be a minister also. He got assigned to the veteran's dorms, but he'll be over here quite a bit. Then I got another friend from Union whose going to preach. He's down at the junior college right now, but he'll be up here for his junior and senior year."

"You're going to be one of the leaders of our class because you have so much experience already," Walter said. "I bet most of the boys in our class probably haven't preached their first sermon yet.

"One thing I need to tell you," I said. "I got a job in the cafeteria starting the fire under the stove. I'll be getting up real early in the morning."

"That's okay with me," Walter said. "I get up about five every morning to read my Bible. So you won't be bothering me at all."

I finally placed my suitcase on the bed and began to take my clothes out and place them in a dresser drawer next to my bed.

"What time is your first class?" I asked while still unpacking my suitcase.

"Nine o'clock," Walter said. "I have Negro History. I already have my textbook for history." He grabbed a book that had been on the floor next to his bed. He held it in the air so I could see it. "It's by Carter G. Woodson. He's a real scholar, writing books and all. He also started Negro History Week."

"Yeah, I know," I said. "We studied him in high school. Prof. Sims actually knows him personally."

"Who is Prof. Sims?" Walter asked.

"He was my teacher back at Sims High School in Union. He is quite a scholar and a man who doesn't bow down to white folks."

"You mean there is a Negro in South Carolina who doesn't bow down to white folks. I'd like to meet him."

I smiled. "You will because I'm sure he'll be down here to visit. And by the way, there are a lot of Negroes who don't bow down to white folks right in Union."

"I believe this is going to be a very interesting first year." Walter said.

"I agree and I'm really looking forward to it. I have to get back over to the chapel. I'm hoping I can meet the Chaplain this morning."

"I'll see you when you get back." Walter fluffed his pillow, lay back on the bed and opened his Bible

"Sure will." I finished and headed out the bedroom.

The Life of Reverend James W. Sanders

Brinnnggg! The piercing sound of my alarm clock broke the silence and brought me straight up in my bed. I turned on the light on the stand next to my bed and glared at the time. It read four o'clock. I climbed out of the bed and glanced over at Walter who was still sound asleep. Evidently the alarm clock did not bother him. That was a good sign because I didn't want the early hour that it went off to become a problem between the two of us. If I had a choice in the matter, the alarm wouldn't go off until seven since my first class wasn't until nine. But no doubt Reverend Bates would be waiting for me, and I took it as a challenge when he questioned if I could do the job. If I got up at four in the morning I figured I would have no problem getting into the bathroom. There were eighteen of us sharing the same facility, and that could become a major problem if all of us headed for the bathroom at the same time.

In an attempt to be as quiet as possible, I tip toed out of the room and then hurried down the hall to the bathroom. My calculation was right. It was open. It seemed strange and I felt a little uncomfortable knowing I had to share the bathroom with seventeen other people. It had been bad enough having to fight with Grady in the morning back home for the bathroom. I could just imagine what it would be like in a couple hours when the others would climb out of bed and get ready for classes. However, that was not my problem. All I had to worry about was getting in and out so I could be there to start that fire on time. As I closed the door and began to clean up, that was the only thought running through my mind.

As I expected, Reverend Bates was waiting for me when I walked into the cafeteria.

"You're fifteen minutes early," he said. "That's what I like to see in my workers. Come on let's get this fire started." He got up and headed toward the oven. "These students going to come in here hungry and rushing to finish registering."

I followed him over to the stove.

"Get them logs," he said and pointed to a pile of logs back against the wall.

I grabbed three nice size logs and carried them over to the stove. I took one and placed it inside the bottom part of the oven.

I was about to place the second one inside when I felt Reverend Bates grip on my arm.

"Hold up," he said. "It's important how you put the second log in. You want to make sure they can breathe for the purpose of a nice strong fire."

I stood back up, still holding the two logs.

"Here, give me that one," he said.

I handed him the log he pointed to. He then placed the log inside the stove.

"Now give me the other one," he instructed.

I did as he asked and handed him the other log. He then placed it inside.

"Now you want to make sure how you get the logs to burning." He struck a match and applied the fire to the log. I watched as the fire started to burn.

"Think you can do that," he asked.

"Yes sir, I'm pretty sure I can."

"Good, cause tomorrow it's on you," he said. "Now your only job is to stay right here and make sure the fire doesn't go out for some reason. You stay until seven and then you can eat."

Two of the cooks strolled into the cafeteria and made their way to the kitchen.

"Check your fire," Reverend Bates said.

I opened the door to the stove, and the fire was blazing hard and strong.

"No problem," I said. "Looks like a good strong flame."

"Our job is done, now it's up to the cooks. I have to go check on a problem with the lighting in the girl's dorm. You can handle this, just make sure you check on the fire every half hour."

"I got it under control."

"See you in the morning right at five," Reverend Bates said and then headed toward the doorway.

The Life of Reverend James W. Sanders

Malachi and I found two seats near the back of the room in our first class. Right at nine o'clock Dr. Cherry strolled into the room and stood at the podium. He exuded knowledge, determination and confidence. He was the kind of man that you wanted to respect just because of his demeanor. He was the first of many college Professors that I would come to respect. When he spoke, it was with authority.

"Welcome to Benedict College for most of you all. I assume that for many of you this is your first college class. "

No one responded. We all sat there intent on listening and learning.

"This class is designed to teach you about your history. We will examine the period of slavery, reconstruction, and the advent of Jim Crow Laws in a segregated South. We will study those members of our race that have been in the forefront as leaders. Of course we will study Sojourner Truth, Harriet Tubman, and Frederick Douglass, and many of the other abolitionists such as William Lloyd Garrison, and the great United States Senator Charles Sumner who led the fight for passage of the 13th and 15th Amendments to the United States Constitution. And of course we will study the presidency of Abraham Lincoln who was the great emancipator. Without his courageous efforts we might still be caught in the ugly web of slavery."

Dr. Cherry held a textbook up so we all could see it. "This is a history of the Negro written by the great scholar, Carter G. Woodson. You can purchase it in the book store. Everyone should buy it and be prepared to discuss the first chapter by Thursday." Dr. Cherry paused while we wrote down the name and the author of the book. "I have invited Dr. Woodson to visit our school this semester. We are waiting to hear back from him. We have also extended an invitation to Dr. Du Bois to visit with us. There is no man with a better understanding and no man more knowledgeable about our people after emancipation than Dr. Du Bois."

What an honor, I thought, to have such great men visit our campus. I definitely would not miss those lectures. I could only hope that they would not visit on the weekend since I was scheduled to go home every Friday to fulfill preaching commitments. One of the great advantages to attending an all-Negro college was the level of scholars who might visit the campus during the semester. These men might not be viewed as outstanding men at white colleges and universities, and probably wouldn't even be invited to lecture in the South. But to us they were great men with outstanding messages for the students on our campus.

"I will let you leave early today so that you can get over to the book store and purchase your text book," Dr. Cherry said. "Be ready to discuss the first chapter on Thursday. And let me close this morning with a promise that if you study hard, read and discuss the topics important to this class, then you will be much more knowledgeable about your history, and you'll be much more prepared to take on the burdens of equality and liberty for your people in the future, You are dismissed."

I had classes all day on Tuesday and by the end of that first day was excited about Benedict College. I now knew that I had made the best choice for me. I was pleased with what would be my new home for the next four years. I practically ran over to the bookstore to purchase Dr. Woodson's textbook for Dr. Cherry's class.

That semester I learned more about our history in the state of South Carolina than what I had expected. We read about the exploits of Robert Smalls, who right at the beginning of the Civil War commandeered a cargo boat, the *Planter*, right into open waters and presented it as a prize to the United States Navy. Smalls went on to become a Congressman from South Carolina during Reconstruction. Another hero was Joseph Rainey, who also was elected to Congress in 1878. And there was Robert Brown Elliott, also elected to Congress and famous for making one of the most eloquent speeches ever delivered on the floor of the House of Representatives, in the United States Congress. A man of particular interest to me was Robert Cain, who was the first Black clergyman to serve in the Congress. Cain also served as a city alderman, a delegate to the 1868 state constitutional convention, and as a spokesperson for his people. Mr. Cain was proof that a minister could be a spiritual and a social leader at the same time. He was also from South Carolina. In fact, our state led the nation in the number of Black members of Congress, a total of six, from 1878 until the Jim Crow laws took away the right for Black men to vote in 1900. The only other courses that I could imagine would be more interesting than the history of my people would be my religious classes, but they had to wait a couple years.

8.

Benedict turned out to be quite a challenge. Our Professors pushed us and made sure we met the same standard of excellence, as other colleges demanded of their students. Their goal, besides providing us with new and useful knowledge about the world, was to show us that we were just as talented as any students. Early on we came to recognize that the only reason we were not admitted to the larger universities in the state of South Carolina was because of our race and not our intelligence. For that reason alone they were very demanding, and sometimes I questioned whether I could keep up with the work, still study the Bible, and preach on the weekends. Riding back and forth every weekend with Malachi was a lifesaver because we were able to reinforce each other that we could do the job.

My schedule allowed me very little time for a social life. The Benedict college community bustled with activity all the time. Students would walk along Gervais and Oak Streets which were thriving areas on the campus. Other students walked the two blocks to Booker T. Washington High School and volunteered as tutors. I volunteered to tutor in math whenever I could find the time.

I did find time to begin dating. She was a student at Benedict and lived in the Ceila Saxon Apartments with relatives while in school. Her home was in Marion, South Carolina. We met in the middle of the semester my sophomore year, and soon after started dating. Our dates consisted of going to the Carver Movie Theater across the street from the campus. On occasion we would ride with friends over to the Capitol Theater on Heyward Street in downtown Columbia.

We hardly ever spent any time on the weekends since I always came home. Evidently her parents were relatively well off. They owned a tobacco farm in Marion. When we met I had just broken up with Mae Mae Simms who had been my girlfriend throughout high school. As a young nice looking and educated preacher, I was in demand among the girls. It was every mother's dream for her daughter to marry a preacher, and especially an educated one. I believe most of the young girls at Benedict were there to find a husband more than get an education. There were very few educated Black men, and in fact there were more women at Benedict than men. The men on campus had their pick but I was not the kind of man who needed to date more than one girl at a time. For that reason I was loyal to Burch, although she often got on my nerves. Needless to say, I was not serious and did not consider Burch as the woman with whom I would spend the rest of my life. She was a junior and would graduate before me. I figured after she left Benedict that would be the end of our relationship, and I could then find the right woman for me. In the meantime she was good company, and I enjoyed being with her during the weekdays I was on campus.

My most active participation was with the Kirkland Ministerial Union, an organization of students who planned to become ministers. It had been around for over fifty years. The purpose of the organization was to administer to the special needs of students struggling with their studies. We did tutoring, counseling, and would even help raise money for some of the students who came up short with tuition. As one of the advanced ministers, the other students asked me about how it felt to stand before a congregation and deliver a sermon. They asked me was I nervous or did I ever lose my concentration and mess up on my delivery? Since I was already ordained and preached in many different churches, I often felt that I was the oldest member of the group, even though a number of the students were much older than me. Some of them were veterans returning from the war just like Malachi. Often we would gather just to discuss issues relevant to us at the time.

One of our more lively discussions had to do with Jackie Robinson, who in 1947 integrated major league baseball. Many students viewed Robinson's breaking the color barrier in baseball as the beginning of the end to segregation. Others viewed it as nothing more than an anomaly with no bearing on racial prejudice, especially in the south. They argued that it would take a much bigger event to have an impact on entrenched segregation. Bigotry, racism, and segregation were so ingrained in white American thought and behavior, nothing short of God's intervention could end it. Another group of students suggested that change would come only when ministers took the energy to step outside the pulpit and into the streets to assist the radical groups in their fight against segregation. If it meant going to jail, well that is what we would have to do. I didn't like the prospect of going to jail but I was ready to go if necessary. We were also very much aware of Dr. Bacoates feelings on student involvement in social issues. He was adamantly opposed to it, and probably would have suspended students who chose to take a stand. But ultimately our loyalty was to the teachings of Jesus Christ. To stand by and not take a stand would have been inimical to God.

Our involvement in the rapidly changing social and political terrain in South Carolina was the basis of many of our discusssions. Just before Christmas break in 1949, Rufus Jackson, one of the ministerial students from Summerton, South Carolina ran into the dorm with very exciting news.

"I just talked with my Dad and he told me that the Negroes in Summerton just signed a petition of complaint in Federal Court against Clarendon County protesting segregated schools," he shouted.

"What? Are you serious?" A number of us sitting in the lounge responded.

"No, it's true," Rufus replied. "Mr. Thurgood Marshall of the NAACP has been working with some of the local residents. A man named Harry Briggs of Summerton filed on behalf of his son, Harry Briggs, Jr.," Rufus continued with excitement in his voice. "South Carolina is going to be the first state to outlaw segregated schools and we all have to be involved."

"You know we can't get involved," I said. "Dr. Bacoates would expel all of us."

"But there has to be something we can do," Malachi said.

"We can pray for Mr. Marshall not to get lynched," one of the other students sitting next to me added. "Them rednecks in Clarendon County going to take it out on everybody."

"Yeah, you right about that," Rufus said. "The mayor of the city owns a gas station where Mr. Briggs works, and he already fired him and gave him his severance pay which was nothing but a carton of cigarettes. And Mr. Briggs got five children and now no job."

"We may not be able to do anything right now," I said. "But in three years we graduate and we'll all have churches. We have to be prepared to stand up for change that has to come, and desegregation is at the top of the list."

"A good thing they filed in Federal Court cause they sure wouldn't get anywhere in a state or local court," another student added.

"Yeah, but the question's going to be does it belong in Federal Court or will they send it back to the state?" Still another student asked.

"Let's pray that it remains at the federal level. Cause if it doesn't, it's over before it even gets started," I said. "But we still needed to get involved in the racial issues that seem to be building up every year. We need an opportunity."

Every year the Kirkland Ministerial Foundation participated in one of the most important religious programs at Allen College, the Methodist School right across the street from us, Allen College's history goes back to 1870 when the African Methodist Episcopal Church established it in order to educate the newly freed slaves around Cokesbury, South Carolina. It moved from that location to Columbia in 1880 and changed the name from Payne College to Allen in honor of Richard Allen, one of the most important figures in African American religious history and founder of the African Methodist Episcopal Church. We were Baptists and they Methodists but we all realized that we were Negroes with the responsibility to help our people. We worshiped the same Christ and the same God. It made sense for us to visit and exchange views during the school year.

The Allen students always invited us to attend a day dedicated to the writings and preaching's of Reverend Allen. Five Allen students reading a few lines recited one of the more Profound writings by this great man and leader. We sat in the auditorium and took in the printed prayers of Reverend Allen.

The Life of Reverend James W. Sanders

The first student, a freshman, stood at the podium. "We will now read passages from the writings of our founder, Richard Allen. These writings are called, 'Acts of Faith'." He began.

"I believe God, that thou are an eternal, incomprehensible spirit, infinite in all perfections, who didst make all things out of nothing, and dost govern them all by the wise providence. Let me always adore thee with Profound humility, as my Sovereign Lord; and help me to love and praise thee with godlike affections, and suitable devotions."

The first student stopped, turned and strolled back to his place, and the second student, a sophomore, sauntered up to the podium.

"I believe that in the unity of the Godhead there is a trinity of persons, that thou art perfectly one and perfectly three; one essence and three persons. I believe O Blessed Jesus, that thou art of one substance with the Father, the very and eternal God, that thou didst take upon thee our frail nature, that thou didst truly suffer, and were crucified, dead and buried, to reconcile us to the Father, and to be a sacrifice for sin."

The second student turned and returned to his position in the line and the third student, a junior, took his place at the podium.

"I believe, that according to the types and prophecies which went before of thee, and according to thy own infallible prediction, thou didst by thy own power rise from the dead the third day, that thou didst ascend into Heaven, that there thou sittest on thy throne of glory adored by angels, and interceding for sinners. I believe, O Lord, that thou hast not abandoned me to the dim light of my own reason, to conduct me to happiness; but that thou hast revealed in the Holy Scriptures whatever is necessary for me to believe and practice, in order to my eternal salvation."

He ended his reading and a senior strolled up to the podium.

"O how noble and excellent are thy precepts; how sublime and enlightening the truth; how persuasive and strong the motives; how powerful the assistance of thy holy religion, in which thou hast instructed me; my delight shall be in thy statutes, and I will not forget thy word."

The student paused while the ushers in the aisles passed out a passage to all of us sitting in the audience. The student then instructed us. "Please read together the final passage from this great man's adoration of our Father in Heaven."

We all read together, "I believe it is my greatest honor and happiness to be thy disciple; how miserable and blind are those that live without God in the world, who despise the light of thy holy faith. Make me to part with all the enjoyments of life; nay, even life itself, rather than forfeit this jewel of great price. Blessed are the sufferings, which are endured, happy are the death, which is undergone for Heavenly and immortal truth. I believe that thou hast prepared for those that love thee, everlasting mansions of glory; if I believe thee, O eternal happiness."

Once the reading ended and the senior took his place behind the podium, the Allen choir stood and sang, *Amazing Grace.* That topped off an amazing morning of entertainment. We returned to Benedict completely satisfied that our God was in control of all things and that change would eventually come. And once it gained momentum no one, not even the devil, could stop it. Visiting Allen was always a spiritual and uplifting event for me.

Those first two years at Benedict, most of my activity was away from the college back home in Union. I was practically preaching at some small church out in the country every Sunday. Then my big opportunity came when Bethel Baptist in Kelton, South Carolina called me to be their pastor. At nineteen years old, I had my first church. Kelton was out in the country about six miles from Union. The members of Bethel were sharecroppers who did not have a lot of money but had a lot of faith that God would eventually deliver them out of a life of misery and poverty. Their only relief from the cruelty of life was the church and that made my job critical to their happiness. They were very poor and could not offer me a salary, but would pay with a collection they took up at the end of the service.

During my first few months as the pastor I didn't own a car. Poppa let me drive his Chevrolet every Sunday to the service. It was a hectic schedule. I had to drive out there and get back to Union in order to catch my ride with Malachi back to Benedict. I still had my job lighting the fire under the stove.

After six months as pastor, God sent me a gift. One of the mechanics in town offered to sell his 1943 Pontiac to me on a monthly payment plan. The church began to take up a separate collection in order to help pay for the car. I no longer had to depend on using Poppa's car to get out to Kelton, and I now began to drive Malachi to Benedict in my vehicle. We traded off on weeks.

My schedule had become so hectic I hardly had any time for Burch. She had no problem letting me know she was not happy with our relationship. To be quite honest I wasn't that happy with it either. But I wasn't ready to let her go so I made a concession and promised to drive down to Marion on the weekend and meet her family. I convinced Malachi to go with me since his wife was going out of town that weekend. We planned to drive to Marion on Saturday morning, spend the night, get up early Sunday and be back in Union for church services.

I was at Malachi's house by six in the morning and we left Union just a little after the hour. We drove our usual route through Newberry to Columbia. We followed the highway through Camden, a city full of antebellum homes. Just as we came into Lee County, I burst out in laughter.

Malachi glanced over at me, "What's so funny?" He asked.

"When I was in the tenth grade, Prof. Sims made us students memorize all the counties in South Carolina for a geography test," I said. "We had to sing them in a song similar to the alphabet song, and we had to get them right or else he instituted corporal punishment on our behinds."

"Do you still know them all?" He asked

"You better believe I do. I made sure I memorized them so that I wouldn't be the victim of the paddle. Latta and I were in competition to see who would get the paddle."

"Did Latta get the paddle?"

"No way, he memorized them all. I think losing to me would have been more painful than the paddle."

We sped by the sign that read.

WELCOME TO BISHOPVIILLE, SOUTH CAROLINA.

"Rumor has it that people spotted a huge reptile monster right here in Bishopville," I said changing the subject.

"Yeah and there is suppose to be a million dollar reward for anyone who can capture it," Malachi added.

"They call it the lizard man, and if we see it, you want to go for the million dollars?" I asked.

"Why not, what we got to lose?" Malachi said.

"Maybe our lives."

"In that case, I think I'll pass it up." We looked at each other momentarily and laughed.

We were making good time as we passed through Florence County into Marion County. This was my second trip down into this part of the sate. I had traveled with Reverend Zimmerman to Mullins where he preached at Second Baptist Church. When we drove into the city all the warehouses were full of tobacco and the entire city smelled of tobacco. It still had that same smell now as Malachi and I passed through.

It was a little after ten in the morning when we arrived in Marion. Burch had given me directions to her parent's farm. It was located on the outskirts of the town in a place called Centenary. It was quite an operation; one that you usually don't associate with someone of color. Evidently, her family inherited land after slavery, and were able to keep it despite the number of Negroes who lost property because of the Black Codes and the Ku Klux Klan. Often when a Negro farmer did well, white farmers living in his vicinity would burn his crops, sometimes burn his home, and then on occasion actually lynch him for being successful. Burch's family had figured a way to get around all those possible perils to success.

Burch ran out of the house and into the driveway when we pulled in. She stood next to the car as we got out. Even though we were considered boyfriend and girlfriend we shook hands instead of hugging. She also shook hands with Malachi.

"You all hungry?" She asked.

"No, not right now," I said. "We ate a big breakfast before leaving Union."

She swung the screen door open and waved us inside.

"Come on in. Mamma and Daddy are in the living room."

We stood there and waited for her to take the lead, then followed her into the living room.

"Daddy, Mamma, this is James Sanders and his friend Malachi Duncan," she said.

Her parents remained seated as we walked over, shook his hand and bowed politely to her mother.

"Thank you for the invitation to visit with your daughter," I said.

"I understand you're a preacher," her father said ignoring my thanking them.

"Yes sir, ordained in 1946 by Reverend A.C. Duncan in Union, South Carolina," I answered. "Reverend Duncan is the father of my best friend here, Malachi, who is also a preacher."

There was silence as I waited for them to respond. I knew they would be impressed with two young men attending Benedict with their chosen career in the ministry.

"I guess since you at Benedict and not Allen you both going to be Baptist ministers," he said.

"That's right," I said. "We both have deep roots in the Baptist church. My grandfather is the President of the Deacon Board at Corinth and of course Malachi's father is a Baptist preacher and also President of the PACOLET association of Baptist ministers in Union."

"Do you young men plan to stay in the South or will you do like a lot of our young educated men, and leave for the north?" He asked.

"No sir," Malachi now spoke up. "I had the opportunity to spend some time in New York after I got out of the army and didn't like it."

"You served your country in the war?" He asked, this time looking directly at Malachi.

"Yes I did," Malachi answered. "And when I got out I visited my brother who lives in New York. Sometimes we folks here in the south get the idea that our people up North are doing so much better than we are, but that's not the truth."

"*The Chicago Defender* newspaper was responsible for a lot of folks leaving the South," Burch's father said. "Before you all's time they used to ship that paper all over South Carolina and other places urging Negroes to leave their home and go up North cause things were so much better. But the white folks up there aren't any different than the ones down here. They going to try to take advantage of the Negro too." He paused and shifted his position on the couch. His wife sat there staring more at me than Malachi. I guess she was trying to size me up, since I was the one supposed to be dating her daughter. "Only difference is you don't have as much segregation and hatred up there as you do down here."

"I believe you are right sir," I said.

"Daddy, I'm going to take James and Malachi to the market. I want to prepare a very special meal for them," Burch said.

"Good, good," Burch's father said. He got up from the couch. "You do that and I'm going to get out to the fields. You boys enjoy yourself while you're here in Marion." He turned and with a slight limp strolled out of the room.

"I hope you young men do enjoy yourself while you are our guests," Burch's mother finally said. "We're going to prepare a special meal for you all that'll make you always remember your trip down here." She also got up and followed behind her husband out of the room.

"Mama I need to talk to you before we leave," Burch said and sauntered out of the room leaving us standing there. "I'll be right back," she turned and looked back at us before she disappeared into the other room.

"What you think, Dunc?" We both sat down on the couch.

"Seem like pretty good people," Malachi said. "But you can't tell much about folks in such a short period of time. I did notice that her mother was staring you up and down. Must have made you a little nervous."

"Not really, I'm used to being stared at."

"But not by your girlfriend's mother."

"It just ain't that serious, Dunc."

"You know they were waiting for you to ask permission to court their daughter?"

"Like I said, it just isn't that serious. No way can I get serious about a girl this far from Union. And them folks at the church going to be looking for me to marry one of the local girls. You know how our folks are. The minister, if he's single, got to marry one of the eligible girls in the church."

"But Bethel isn't the church that you going to be ministering to once you graduate."

"You're probably right, and that's more reason why I can't get that serious with Burch. When I do get my permanent church, I know there's going to be plenty young ladies I can consider for a wife." I paused for a second and looked all around me. "Don't you get a strange feeling in here?" I asked.

"What you mean?"

"I'm not sure. It just seems kind of different."

We sat there and waited for Burch to return. Silence seemed to be the best choice at the time. I didn't want to say too much for fear someone might walk up on us or worst, be listening.

"Let's go," Burch said as she rushed back into the room. "I'll drive since you all been driving all morning and I know where I'm going."

"Sounds good to me," I said.

"Me too," Malachi agreed.

We walked out of the house, climbed into one of the trucks parked around the back and headed to the market.

The market was located under a large structure with open sides. There were vegetable and fruit stands in long rows on one side of the structure, and meat stands with a large array of steaks, pork chops, and chickens on the other side. It seemed as though half the Negro population of Marion was in the market. Men and women stood in front of the vendors buying different vegetables, fruits and meats. Young kids ran up and down the aisles playing tag, and right outside a bunch of young girls were playing jump rope and jacks. You felt the life and soul of the Negro community right in that place.

We followed behind Burch over to the meat stand.

"Let me have six of those nice size steaks," she said to the lady behind the counter. "And let me have four cut-up chickens."

I smiled and looked at Malachi. I knew our thoughts merged and we knew we would be eating good that night. Hopefully, steaks and not chicken.

Burch paid the lady and then handed two packages to Malachi and me. We followed her over to the vegetable stand. She bought greens, corn, okra and kale. We made our way over to the fruit stand where she bought strawberries, bananas and five nice size sweet potatoes. There was no doubt in my mind that we were in for a grand feast that evening.

We finished our shopping, climbed back into the truck and headed back to the house. Both Malachi and I had wide grins on our face. I was happy that I decided to make the trip. On the drive back Burch told us how close we were to Myrtle Beach and to the Georgetown area. Malachi touched me on my back because we both had heard rumors about voodoo coming out of the gullah and geechie people in the lower part of the state.

As we turned off the main road onto the dirt path that led back to the house, I noticed five cars parked outside. A number of people stood on the porch talking. Burch must have invited her entire family and some neighbors over to meet Malachi and me. Instantly, the comments I had made to Malachi earlier shot through my mind. "It ain't that serious." We got out of the truck and strolled back up to the house. Before we were on the porch an elderly lady glared at us and asked.

"So which of these two men is the one?" She asked.

"Mama Jackson, these are my friends," Burch quickly replied. "I guess I have to say I spend more time with James," she continued and put her hand on my shoulder.

"Hmmh, he a handsome one," Mama Jackson said. "So you the young new preacher at Bethel in Kelton?"

My mouth halfway opened. How did she know that? I hadn't

even told Burch that I was the pastor at Bethel, only that I had been preaching there lately. Evidently, word had spread all the way down to Marion. But why hadn't Burch asked the same question. If her family knew, then she had to know, also.

"Yes ma'am, I am," I answered.

"Burch, you better hang on to this one. He's nice looking and he's a preacher. Can't do no better than that, less it's a doctor. Welcome to the family."

"Ma'am, I am not engaged to Burch," I said without thinking. I didn't want to embarrass Burch but on the other hand, I didn't want to mislead these people thinking I was about to propose to her. I glared over at Malachi, who just shook his head from side to side. I knew exactly what he was thinking. You got yourself into this mess now figure out how you going to get out of it. But it didn't matter how I got into it, bottom line I was not about to propose marriage to Burch. If that's the reason why the entire family was there, well they wouldn't get what they came for.

"You ain't engaged to nobody else are you?" Mama Jackson asked. By now a number of the relatives had surrounded us as she continued to probe.

"No ma'am, I'm not engaged to anyone else. I'm still a student at college and then I'm pastor of a church. I just don't have time to get engaged," I said.

"Dinner 's ready," Burch's mother came out on the porch and announced to us.

I felt relieved that I could get out of this trap. I stared over at Malachi and he grinned.

"I think it appropriate that one of our young ministers lead us in prayer," Burch's father said, as we all sat around a long dinner table.

Malachi and I, along with some of Burch's family members, were seated on one side while Burch, her mother, father, Mama Jackson and some elderly relatives on the other. I turned and looked at Malachi.

"You do it," he whispered.

"Please bow your heads," I said.

I said a very short but appropriate prayer. I didn't want it to be long because I just didn't feel real comfortable with Burch or her family. However, a thick delicious steak could help smooth over the rough edges. With my prayer over, I anticipated the dinner.

Chicken I thought, what happened to the steaks? Again, I looked at Malachi and could tell from his expression he was thinking the same thing. Burch piled our plates with smothered chicken, mashed potatoes, corn, greens and corn bread. She poured us both a tall glass of lemonade. It wasn't that bad a meal after all, even though my mind stayed fixed on those big steaks we had bought earlier at the market.

Half way through the meal I noticed Malachi stopped eating. He put his fork down and just sat there almost in a comatose state.

"You all right?" I asked.

"I don't know," he said. "All of a sudden I feel dizzy and somewhat nauseated."

No one else seemed to notice that Malachi had stopped eating. And if they did, they didn't comment or ask about him. I found that rather strange.

"I need to go," Malachi whispered to me.

"What, right now?" I asked.

"Is something wrong?" Burch's mother finally asked.

"No ma'am," I said. "Malachi just not feeling too good."

"Let's go outside and talk," Malachi said ignoring the others.

"Would you please excuse us for a minute," I said to the family. We got up and hurried outside. I knew this had to appear real strange, but my friend was acting strange also and that was a greater concern to me.

We stood outside near my car.

"What is it?" I asked

"We got to get out of here," Malachi said.

"Why? I mean what's wrong?"

"All of a sudden I got this strange feeling and it's telling me that these folks practice voodoo. I think it was meant for you but it got me."

"What are you talking about? Voodoo!"

"Yes, voodoo, now we got to get out of here. No way I'm spending the night down here."

"Right now, right this minute? Can I finish the meal?"

"I'd suggest you don't. They out for you and if you finish they might get you."

"Why you think they out to get me?" I asked with a great deal of excitement and some trepidation.

"Probably because you haven't asked their permission to date their daughter with the intent to marry her."

"What!"

"Yes, now let's get out of here."

"Okay, but let me go in and give them an excuse for our leaving."

"You do that, but I'm not going back in there."

"I got you. I'll be right back. But if anything crazy happens you have to come back in there and get me," I said, and then headed back inside to confront Burch and her family with this rather strange development.

After fighting off Burch and her family's objections, especially Mamma Jackson, I excused myself, exited the house and we started back to Union. As soon as we were about ten miles away from their house and that meal, Malachi suddenly recuperated. There were no symptoms at all.

"Isn't that strange," he said. "I feel just fine now. No symptoms at all."

"You really believe it was some kind of voodoo?" I asked.

"Absolutely, no doubt," Malachi said. "I know it was. Look at where we're at. It's voodoo in Louisiana, in the Carolinas and in the low country. It's called roots. The closer to the water the better it works. The water carries the spirits. As soon as you get back to Benedict, you'd better break off your relationship with Burch. That girl and her family are into some funny kind of stuff."

I took my eyes off the road long enough to glare over at Malachi.

"You sure all your symptoms are gone?"

"It's like I never had any symptoms at all. I feel nothing."

"I never believed in roots."

"You'd better start, cause you just experienced it with me," Malachi scowled. "That stuff is witchcraft and it's real, but the blood of Jesus can defeat any evil spirits."

Again, I looked over at Malachi and sighed in relief. I knew the first thing I had to do on Monday was be to break off my relationship with Burch. This time I would wait until the right lady came along, the one that I would marry and spend the rest of my life loving. That very special person would come into my life once I became pastor at Bethel Baptist Church in Gaffney, South Carolina

9.

The first call I made Sunday after that disastrous trip to Marion was to Burch letting her know that we would no longer be seeing each other. She blasted me with some very choice words, but it was over and nothing more needed to be said. That same afternoon I received a call from Deacon Nelson Brown, Chairman of the Deacon Board at Bethel Baptist Church in Gaffney inviting me to preach there next week on Easter Sunday. I was elated at the invitation to preach at one of the upcoming churches in upper South Carolina. The first person I told the good news was Grandpa Sanders. He quickly made a couple telephone calls and shared some even better news with me. Evidently Bethel was searching for a new minister. They would be inviting a number of preachers in to test the waters with them. I was third in line. Grandpa emphatically stressed that I do my very best because this was an excellent opportunity for a young preacher. Bethel was a church where I could build my ministry. I couldn't wait for next Sunday. All the way back to Benedict that evening I explored different topics on which to preach with Malachi.

"Dunc, I have to be awfully good next Sunday," I said.

"You don't have to worry. Look at all you got going for you," Malachi said. It was his week to drive so I had my Bible open leafing through different passages. "You're young, you're nice looking, you can sing, something awfully important to a Baptist congregation, and you know your Bible."

"I'm not so sure being young is going to be in my favor," I said as I continued looking through the New Testament.

"I think you're wrong, churches are looking for young preachers that can be with them for a very long time."

"But nineteen, that's awfully young." I sighed.

"Look at it this way," Malachi said and glanced over at me. "They already know your age so that didn't stop them from inviting you to preach. It can't be that important to them."

"I guess you're right, at least I hope you are." I paused and closed the Bible. "You got to be there."

"I know. I already found someone to fill in at my church. I wouldn't miss this for nothing in the world. Is Latta going to make it?"

"I don't know. I wasn't able to get hold of him. I'll call him tomorrow."

"He'll be there if he can make it. After all this is one of the most important days in your life."

"I know and it'll be one of the happiest, also."

It was practically impossible for me to concentrate on schoolwork. I could barely get up in the morning to light the fire. It was extremely cold for April and if it hadn't been for Malachi who had moved over to my dorm and was now my roommate, I probably would have missed getting to the cafeteria on time. All my spare time I spent concentrating on my sermon for Sunday. It wasn't until Wednesday that God answered my prayers and led me to preach from the "Book of Job." Before we had left Union on Sunday, I was able to get sermons on "Job" from Reverend A.C. Duncan and Reverend Zimmerman. I was engrossed in studying their words, cutting and pasting the best from their sermons along with my own words. I had to be good. There was no choice in the matter. I wanted to be the next pastor of Bethel Baptist in Gaffney and I believe God wanted it for me as well. I took the attitude that it was mine to lose. No one could beat me but myself. So it was mandatory that I spend every free minute preparing.

On Thursday I had the opportunity to talk with Dr. Riley. I respected him a great deal. He invited me into his office. I took a seat in front of his large oak desk. He looked at me over the top of his glasses. He reminded me of Prof. Sims.

"You have a great opportunity James," he began the conversation. "Bethel up in Gaffney is a growing church and will soon be a major player among Baptist churches in the state. I hope you are prepared for the tremendous responsibility you'll have to those souls who'll look to you to take care of their every need, not just church needs, but family needs, work needs and just every day life needs if God allows you the opportunity to take that position."

"If they offer it to me, I'll be ready."

"What are you going to do about your education? You're a sophomore now and still have two years to go for your degree."

"I plan to finish my education because I'll need another source of income. I don't believe they'll be able to offer me a full time salary." I stopped. I was acting like I already had the job. I guess that was my confidence. I was self-assured but not cocky. There is a big difference between the two.

He looked relieved. "You're absolutely right. You will need the degree to teach. So whatever happens, make sure you know you have to graduate." Dr. Riley leaned half way across his desk. "James, there is one other important fact that I never want you to forget. As a Baptist preacher you are blessed, but you are not privileged. You can never place yourself above those people who need you. Remember that our people, right after slavery, turned to the church for their salvation and survival. In many ways they are still totally dependent on the church. If you are blessed to get this job don't ever forget your humble beginnings, and always relate that to your congregation. You will, no doubt, have more poor people in your congregation than any others. Be sure to always take very good care of them. Remember our savior tells us how you treat the least of mine is how you treat me."

Listening to this man reminded me of the many times men like Prof. Sims, Reverend Zimmerman, Grandpa and Poppa had offered similar advice. I recognized how fortunate I was to have such men advising me on life. They had lived it, and I was only beginning. With each session I had with one of these men, it became much clearer that I would inherit the same responsibility to guide future generations. My preparation for doing that had begun years ago and still continued to the present. My vision was clear; someday Latta, Malachi and I would assume the leadership mantle in the state of South Carolina for the religious and educational instruction of our people. And of all the advice we had received over the years, the most critical were the words that Dr. Riley had just shared with me; what you do for the least of my people, you do for me.

That week dragged on forever. I was anxious for it to end so that I could get on to the most important sermon I had preached since I was ordained. I spent time researching Bethel Baptist Church in Gaffney. It was considered a progressive church with a good mixture in the congregation. Many of the laborers and blue collar workers as well as well-educated people called Bethel their church home. The church was located in a small city, but it was growing and as a result the attendance at the many local places of worship was also growing. I knew that Prof. Sims preached at Limestone Baptist Church. It was older and bigger than Bethel, but there was more than enough salvation to go around at all the different churches.

My first preference would have been a church right in Union. I knew that might not happen for a very long time and I was anxious for God to provide me with a larger church. The Lord had blessed me at Bethel in Kelton and like the scripture states, "I was faithful and gracious over a few, so I knew that eventually he would bless me with plenty."

Friday morning after I fired up the stove in the cafeteria, I hurried back to the dorm where Malachi was still sleeping. I ran into our room and shook him.

"Let's go," I said. "I need to get on back to Union."

"What's your rush?" Malachi asked as he rubbed the sleep from his eyes. He rose up in the bed. "We'll leave at our usual time around nine o'clock. So just relax." He lay back down and turned his back to me.

I was much too nervous and anxious to relax. I snatched the covers off Malachi.

"Come on, Dunc, we got to get out of here," I said. "No way I can relax when I have so much on my mind about Sunday."

Malachi threw his legs over the side of the bed and jumped to his feet. He rubbed his eyes again and headed out of the room toward the bathroom.

The Life of Reverend James W. Sanders

"All right, all right," he said as he disappeared out of the room.

I sat in the passenger's seat studying my sermon for Sunday. Malachi had driven that week so it gave me the opportunity to use the travel time to work on perfecting my delivery. I momentarily allowed my thoughts to wander off the paper in front of me. If offered the position at Bethel, my prayers would be answered. I wanted nothing more than to be obedient to God and do His will. It had been instilled in me over the years that it was never about what I wanted, but what God wanted. Both Malachi and Latta felt the same way. If the three of us did God's will, then someday we would pastor major congregations and bring souls to Christ.

The Holy Spirit had already confirmed to me that my future lay right in my home state, but I could also make a difference worldwide right from there. Hopefully, I could contribute some aspect of the changes that were destined to come during my lifetime. I recalled the discussion Prof. Sims had with the class when we questioned him about the terrible discrepancy in a law that would allow prisoners of war to eat where American citizens were not allowed. He told us that change was inevitable, and that we must participate when the time came. If I was blessed with a ministry in Gaffney, that is the place where I would diligently work for that change.

"You think you'll ever leave the South?" I asked as I turned and looked at Malachi.

"I don't know," he said. "I been to a lot of places over the past few years because of the war, and right now I can't think of a better place than right here."

"Even with all the problems?"

"Even with all the problems. There's going to be problems wherever you go. And these fields are our roots. Right here in South and North Carolina is where we grew a culture. Our people struggled for survival right in these fields." He paused and stuck his hand out the window, pointing to the fields all around us.

A farmer, who happened to look up just as Malachi stuck his arm out the window, waved back at us.

"See that's what I'm talking about," he continued. "That's the kind of spirit we have down here. That farmer automatically waved back as a gesture of friendship. Despite all his hardships, he felt compelled to wave back. It's a camaraderie that stems from hundreds of years of having to stick together. You don't get that but right here in the South, and you sure don't get it up North where everybody is out to beat each other out of whatever they have."

"I know what you mean. If the Lord blesses me with Bethel, I believe I'll spend the rest of my life in that one church."

"You never know what else might be there for you. You have to go wherever the Lord sends you." Malachi paused as if he had to gather his thoughts for what was coming next. "There is an old saying that a man once told the Lord of his plans for the rest of his life and the Lord just laughed. Point is you never know what the man upstairs has for you in the future."

"I can always pray and it may be God's will for me to just stay right there in Gaffney, South Carolina at that one church until I die." I finished and laid my head back on the headrest. "Yes, I'll be content to do the Lord's work in the halls of that church."

"Hurry up Nette," I shouted at my sister Marionette. She was home for Easter break and agreed to travel with me over to Gaffney for the sermon. I was up and ready to go by nine o'clock in the morning. It was about a forty-five minute ride to Gaffney from Union. I figured if we left at nine I would be at the church one hour before the morning service. Now, Marionette was throwing a monkey wrench into my plans. I had to go, and she was still in the bathroom doing what females do and that is piddle with her hair.

"Nette, come on," I shouted this time. "We need to leave."

Marionette opened the bathroom door and strolled out into the hall.

"James, you got plenty of time. It isn't but a forty-five minute drive to Gaffney, so were good on time."

"You never know what can happen, and there is no way I can be late."

"Okay, James go start the car and I'm on my way."

The Life of Reverend James W. Sanders

As I started toward the door, Mamma and Poppa both met me in the hall way.

"Good luck James," Mamma said.

"Preach as God directs you," Poppa said. "We know you going to do just fine. That church is going to be yours. God has already made that decision. So just relax, preach and meet your new congregation."

I hugged both Mamma and Poppa, and sauntered out of the house. I said a prayer just as I got into the car. This particular prayer was for me to remain calm and not allow my blood to rise while I waited for Nette.

At the last minute Grady decided he was going to go also. That slowed us down but finally a little after nine we started up Highway 55 to Gaffney.

"You nervous?" Grady asked. He broke the silence.

"About what?" I asked with an air of confidence. I didn't want to let him or Nette know that I was nervous.

"You gotta be a little nervous." Grady continued to probe.

"I told you I'm not nervous. I've preached enough sermons now that I am past getting nervous," I said.

"Don't matter," he continued. "You haven't ever faced a congregation that's going to decide if they're going to hire you."

"I did at Bethel in Kelton."

"That church is so small it doesn't even matter."

"Grady, leave me alone. Let me concentrate," I snapped.

"Told ya, you was nervous," he said and then leaned back in his seat.

"What you going to sing?" Nette asked.

"Don't know yet," I said.

"I have a pretty good idea what it'll be," Grady sounded off from his reared back position.

"No you don't," I retorted. "I'll just wait and see what the Lord sends to me at that moment."

"Remember when we were kids," Nette said. "You used to always play the role of the preacher when we acted out a funeral."

"Yeah, I guess I was rehearsing for the real thing." I glanced at a sign on the side of the road that read 10 miles to Gaffney. My future was only ten miles away, I thought. "What time is it, Nette?"

" A little past nine-thirty. We're less than a half hour away."

"Now you starting to get nervous." Grady said.

"No, Grady, I'm not getting nervous. What is it with you?"

"Just messing with you, big brother."

"I can do without the harassment," I scowled a little. "I need your support not your harassment."

"Big brother you know you got that," Grady said just as the car began to sputter.

"What's wrong?" Nette asked.

"I don't know. Why of all times would this happen?"

"The devil is busy today," Nette said. "He doesn't want you to get to Bethel."

I pulled the car over to the curb just as the engine died.

"The devil may be hard at work, but I can guarantee you he won't win this battle with the Lord," I said and pointed to a gas station right across the street.

"Are they open?" Grady asked.

"They sure are," I said as I got out of the car and started across the street. I prayed that the man inside the station would be a mechanic who knew something about cars.

I hurried inside and made my plea with the mechanic.

"Sir, my car broke down right across the street. We're from Union and on our way to Bethel Baptist Church here in Gaffney. I was hoping that you could help me out."

"What you think is wrong with it? Did you run out of gas?" He asked.

A tinge of irritation shot through me. Did he think I was dumb enough to not have gas in my car? But I had to squelch that emotion. I needed this man's help.

"No sir, I have plenty gas. If you could help me I can pay," I replied. "You see, I'm preaching this morning at Bethel Baptist Church in Gaffney, and I need to get there on time. So if you could see your way free to help a messenger of the Lord get to the church, I would be much appreciative. Would you help me?"

"You look awfully young to be a preacher?"

Once again that irritation invaded my space and I was inclined to tell this man that God doesn't set any age limits on his messengers. But instead I said.

"I know, I guess I was just blessed."

"Well, ain't no way I can turn down helping a man of God who is blessed." He walked outside and across the street with me. When we reached the car he said, "Pop the hood and let me take a look. Hopefully it's nothing serious and I can fix it right here."

Not hopefully, I thought, but prayerfully.

All the time he was working under the hood I was praying outside the hood. I signaled for Nette and Grady to also pray. After each prayer I looked at my watch. It was getting close to ten o'clock. We were only about five to ten minutes from the church. If he could get it to start within the next half hour, we would be there in plenty of time.

"I think I found the problem," the mechanic said. "But I have to go back over to the station and see if I have the part you need."

I watched as he hurried back across the street. It was time for another prayer. The devil was really testing my endurance. But I knew there was no way that God would let him win, and we would get the car started in time.

Five minutes later the mechanic returned with the part in his hand.

"I think this will do the job," he said and leaned back over the fender with his head inside the hood.

He stayed in that posture for about five minutes, then leaned up and said. "Give it a try."

I got back in the drivers seat, stuck the key in the ignition, closed my eyes and turned it. The engine sputtered, stammered and finally kicked on.

"Yeah, all right," both Nette and Grady shouted. "Praise the Lord, the devil looses again."

"Praise the Lord, he sure does," I said as I got out of the car and pulled some dollars out of my pocket.

The attendant raised his arm toward me. "No charge young man," he said. "Just say a prayer for me while you doing your sermon. I can use all the help I can get, and especially from a man of God."

"Thank you, sir," I practically shouted. "You will not only be in my prayers but the prayers of the entire congregation."

We pulled into the church parking lot right at ten o'clock. There was a young man directing cars to parking spaces. The entire lot was full. I rolled down my window and said.

"I'm Reverend James W. Sanders, your guest preacher for the day."

"Oh, yes sir, Reverend Sanders, follow me I have a special parking space reserved for you."

I rolled the window back up and glared over at Nette. "A special parking space for me," I said.

"You already becoming an important man." She smiled.

I also smiled as I followed the man to a parking space right in front of the church. It was the permanent space reserved for their minister. As I parked the car, I imagined that being my parking place for a long time into the future.

10.

The sweet sounds of *"Precious Lord take my hand. Lead me on, let me stand,"* filled the church as I strolled into the sanctuary with Deacon Nelson Brown and took my seat right behind the pulpit. He sat up there with me. The church was packed. I looked out into the congregation for Nette and Grady. They were sitting in the back of the church. At the last minute, my friends Latta and Malachai couldn't make it over to Gaffney. Since it was Easter Sunday, I knew there would be a large turnout, but I never imagined that there would be standing room only. That fact added to the tinge of nervousness I felt as we took our seats.

Staring out into the congregation as the choir sang, *"I am weak and you are strong, Lead me on Precious Lord,"* I felt proud for my people. Men, women and children were immaculately dressed. Church ladies in straw hats and colorful dresses, and men in dark suits filled the pews. It was a beautiful sight. I prayed that I was up for the occasion. My people deserved the very best and they were looking to me to give that to them. I was confident that once the other activities were out of the way and I began my sermon, the nervousness would disappear and the words necessary to give these magnificent people a sermon worthy of their very special nature, would flow through me from God.

The choir finished its version of "Precious Lord" and then went into a second presentation. I looked back at them just as a lady wearing a red hat and dressed in a red suit with red shoes sauntered from her place in the choir to the front and took the mike. She immediately lifted the spirits of the congregation as she began to sing.

"What a friend we have in Jesus

All our sins and grieves to bear

What a privilege to carry

Everything to God in prayer, "

She paused long enough to stroll right up to the end of the stage. She now stood in front of me. I could observe all of her movements as well as those of the congregation. A number of women immediately jumped up and clapped to the rhythm of the music. The singer continued to raise the level of energy in the church. She turned and looked back at the deacon and me, then turned and faced the congregation.

"Oh what peace we often forfeit

Oh what needless pain we bear

All because we do not carry

Everything to God in prayer. "

The beauty of it all gave me a natural high. I was high on God, and I was high on my people as I watched and listened to them praise the Lord in their own unique way.

Both men and women were on their feet clapping and swaying to the music. One older lady began to dance where she stood as she knocked her hat from her head. It was contagious, as two other ladies followed her lead and also began to dance in place. For a few minutes the drums, the organ, and the piano played in a repetitious beat, creating an even higher crescendo of joy. Deacon Brown, sitting next to me, jumped to his feet and began to clap. The entire congregation was caught up in the joy spreading throughout the sanctuary on this Easter Sunday. I wanted to jump up also but thought it best to wait my turn to fire up the church.

After about fifteen minutes of singing, dancing and rejoicing the choir brought the song to an end. But even as the lead singer returned to her place, the drummer continued to perform to the joy of the congregation. Then the organist kicked back in. Bethel Baptist Church was having a service of love and rejoicing. It went on for another ten minutes before Deacon Brown got up and stood at the pulpit. He brought it to a close but not before adding a portion of the deacon's own prescription for the morning service. Sounding much like the great James Cleveland, he began.

"I'm a soldier in the army of the Lord.

"I thank God that I'm a soldier in the army of the Lord.

"I'm a mighty, mighty soldier in the army of the Lord.

"Got a sword in my hand and got my war clothes on.

"I'm going to ride on

"I'm going to ride on

"In the army of the Lord

"Hallelujah, hallelujah," the congregation responded as the deacon warmed up to the occasion. The support from the congregation gave the deacon a new burst of energy.

"I'm going to walk on

"I'm going to walk on

"In this army

"I'm fighting til I die

"In the army of the Lord"

Deacon Brown paused. One of the great traditions of the Baptist Church was the call and response. The ministers called out to the congregation and waited for their response. It was a tactic used to make sure the entire congregation was involved in the service. It was one of the first lessons learned by any Baptist preacher. Reverend Zimmerman had not only taught me how to utilize call and response, but often would demonstrate it during his sermons. I instantly understood what Deacon Brown was doing. He was determined to keep the congregation at a high level of involvement. I appreciated what he was doing because when I finally stood before them I knew they would be ready for a young fiery preacher to deliver the word.

"My mother is a soldier," he continued.

"My father is a soldier

"I'm a true born soldier

"In the army of the Lord.

"Are you glad to be a soldier

"Got my Bible in my hand

"In the army of the Lord."

He paused and finally ended with, *"What could wash away my sins. Nothing but the blood of Jesus."*

For the next forty-five minutes I sat patiently while the children performed an Easter program, they took collection, had an altar call and then finally Deacon Brown strolled to the pulpit.

"This morning, we are blessed to have a young South Carolina preacher who I know is going to deliver a message straight from God. This is a young man who gave his life to Christ at the young age of fifteen. He was ordained by Reverend A.C. Duncan at the age of sixteen and is now a college student at Benedict in Columbia. He has come here to Gaffney to bring the word of the Lord. So church folk, the next voice you hear will be that of Reverend James W. Sanders from Union, South Carolina."

As I rose and strolled to the pulpit all kinds of thoughts shot through my head. The most dominant one was that I had to give the best sermon in my short lifetime as a preacher. I looked out over the congregation and accepted the awesome responsibility in front of me for the next half hour. My first response once I placed my Bible at the podium was to bow my head and say a short silent prayer for God to deliver me. While praying I could feel all eyes on me as they waited.

"That's all right Brother, take your time," I heard from someone in the congregation.

Those words, I knew, were sent from God through whoever it was that uttered them. I instantly felt relieved and all the tension I felt moments ago was gone. God would, indeed, deliver me. Now the thoughts were racing through my mind at a great speed. I lifted my head, looked out into the people and followed God's lead.

"Traveling Shoes on, Lord," I began to sing this classic Black Baptist gospel song, one that I had adopted as my own. *"Traveling Shoes on, Lord."*

"Got my traveling shoes and I can travel now.

"I feel like traveling, yes, I feel like traveling."

"All right now, young preacher," I heard Deacon Brown say from behind me.

"I don't know what he is to you but he's all right with me." I sang.

"He's all right with me too," a female voice said from the congregation.

The congregation began clapping to the rhythm as the organists, piano player and the man on the drums joined in. I was now warming up to the occasion.

"Been down the road and I started to walk.

"Buckled up my shoes and I started to walk.

"Walking for Jesus.

"Traveled over hills, traveled over mountains, traveled for Jesus."

"If you're ready to travel for Jesus, let me hear you say amen." I was in control. It was time for call and response. "If you ready to buckle up your traveling shoes and join the army of the Lord, let me hear you say amen."

The congregation shouted a chorus of amen. I heard a mixture of men and women. I was about ready to preach as I had never preached before. The fire was burning deep inside my soul and the Holy Ghost had stepped in while James Sanders stepped out.

"If you got your traveling shoes, let me hear an amen." My words were crisp and sharp. "Turn to your neighbor and tell them that I got my traveling shoes on, and I'm enlisting in the army of the Lord. I'm ready to fight for freedom in the army of the Lord."

With confidence I watched as the entire congregation turned to someone next to them and repeated my words. It was now time and I was ready to deliver the sermon that would bring me to Bethel Baptist as their permanent minister.

At some point during the sermon I no longer was in control. The Holy Ghost filled me with words and phrases that penetrated the very essence of that church on Easter Sunday, and half way through my sermon I believe half the congregation was on their feet clapping and shouting. Because it was Easter I preached from "Job" but ended on the last three days of Jesus' life with a standard Baptist denouement to a sermon and that is the crucifixion, the burial in the cave, and the resurrection on the third day. Before sitting down I had to close with praises for Jesus through song.

"It's good to know Jesus.

"Everybody ought to know Jesus.

"He's the lily of the valley

"A bright and morning star

"Everybody ought to know Jesus

"He's the maker, the beginning and the end."

Suddenly I heard the voices of the choir as they stood and joined in. Together we sang.

"He's my all in all

"In the book of Galatians, He's the one who set us free

"In the book of Philippians, He's the one who set us free

"It's good to know Jesus; it's good to know the Lord."

I was so high on the Holy Ghost that I didn't pay much attention to what was happening all around me in that church at that moment. Most of the congregation was on its feet, many standing in the aisles clapping and some were dancing. Another group had come right up to the front of the pulpit and stretched their arms in the air waving back and forth. There was no doubt that the Holy Spirit occupied Bethel Baptist and I had served as the conduit to all the energy at work in that sanctuary.

Finally, the emotions in the sanctuary calmed down, I was able to get everyone back into their seats, and extended the invitation for those seeking a church home to come forward. That morning two families, one consisting of five and the other of six, joined church. As they came forward down the aisles and the deacons welcomed them I knew my chances of becoming the minister at Bethel increased. Eleven new members was proof of my abilities to bring new recruits to the Lord, and specifically to Bethel. It was a growing church and I believed the Deacons knew it could continue to grow with me in the pulpit.

After closing out the service with a prayer, I followed Deacon Brown and the other Deacons to the front of the church, and stood at the door as members lined up to greet and thank me for the sermon. The line extended from the door all the way back to the pulpit. I shook more hands than I'd ever done before. I hugged more old ladies, and on occasion received a kiss on the cheek from or gave a kiss on the cheek to more young and old ladies than I imagined would ever have happened. On numerous occasions I was informed that soon I would have to find a first lady for the church if selected to be the minister. A number of the ladies let me know that they had daughters, who were God-fearing women and members of Bethel, and would fit that role quite well. They emphasized the fact that they were members of Bethel and that led me to believe they expected me to marry from within the church, if I was selected to be their pastor. I heard that suggestion so many times it registered quite well with me.

It was after three o'clock before Nette, Grady and I finally got back on the road to Union. We rode in silence for about five minutes and I knew they were playing a game with me. They were very much aware that I was waiting for them to give me an assessment of my performance. They waited to see if I would break the silence and ask for their opinion. I finally accommodated them.

"Well, what are you waiting for?" I asked in an indirect way.

"What you talking about?" Grady asked. They both snickered.

"You know what I'm talking about?" I snapped. It was like we were kids once again, and the oldest and youngest teamed up against the middle sibling. But this was not a game. My future was at stake and I wanted to know what the two closest persons in my life thought.

"Okay, you were outstanding," Nette finally said. "I didn't know how good you were until today. That church is going to be yours and for a very long time."

"Yeah, you preached today brother," Grady joined in. "That church was rocking from the minute you walked up to the pulpit until the time you sat back down. And you got eleven new members."

"But remember Deacon Brown introduced me as that young preacher, emphasizing the young part," I said as my own doubts took over.

"Don't mean a thing brother," Grady said. "Once you started preaching nobody paid any attention to your age. You sounded like a real polished man of God."

"Grady's right, age won't be a factor in their decision. I heard all those women talking about you marrying their daughters. They know the church is going to offer you that job, and they're getting the first bid in for their daughters."

"Deacon Brown told me they got two more preachers to hear before they make their decision," I said.

"James, don't worry," Nette said. "They will offer you the job so get ready to move to Gaffney, South Carolina. That's going to be your new home. Get ready brother, cause God wants you there."

We rode in silence the rest of the way home. I think we all were exhausted from the excitement of the day, starting with the engine trouble and right up to the last person whose hand I shook after the service. I had to, however, get my second wind. After dinner I still had to conduct a night service at my other Bethel in Kelton.

11.

As soon as I sat down in the passenger's seat of Malachi's car, the drilling began. My car was in the shop for repairs so he agreed to drive for that week. I relaxed back and closed my eyes. Sunday had been extremely exhausting, and I needed to rest during the ride back to Benedict. But Malachi was having no part of it.

"How did it go?" He asked as we hit Highway 251. "Do you think you did good enough to land the job? It would be quite an accomplishment for someone only nineteen years old..."

I kept my head resting back on the headrest with my eyes closed. "I believe the Lord is going to give me my ministry right there," I said.

"What did you preach on?" He asked

"What does every preacher preach about on Easter Sunday?"

"I'm not sure what all preachers chose as their subject on Easter," he answered curtly.

"You preached yesterday didn't you?" I asked him.

"Yeah."

"What did you preach on? I continued my questioning.

"On the resurrection.. How about you?"

"On "Job" and the resurrection."

We looked at each other and laughed.

Malachi nudged me and I came straight up in the bed. I then jumped out of the bed and stared over at the clock. It was already after five o'clock and I was going to be late getting over to the cafeteria to start the fire.

"Oh great Jesus," I shouted. "Reverend Bates is going to choke me." I grabbed my clothes and put them on.

"Aren't you going to wash up first?" Malachi asked.

"Have to do it when I get back," I said as I tied my shoes. "You know everybody's going to be angry with me if that fire isn't up and blazing and the food cooked when they get over there for breakfast."

"You got that right," Malachi said.

I finished lacing my shoes, jumped up and shot out the door.

"See you in an hour."

The fire was already blazing when I walked into the cafeteria. Reverend Bates stood over it, stoking it with the iron.

"Sorry, sir," I said as I approached the stove.

"First time in over two years, that ain't bad at all," Reverend Bates said without looking up. He had the fire really blazing and shooting straight up.

"This past weekend was hectic," I explained in an effort to create an acceptable excuse. "I preached my trial sermon at Bethel in Gaffney and then later that evening had to preach my sermon in Kelton."

"How did you do?" He asked.

"I feel I did quite well."

"When are they going to let you know?"

"They got two more preachers to try out, then they'll make a decision."

Reverend Bates finished stoking the fire and handed me the iron.

"No doubt they going to chose you," he said. "You young, nice looking, you sing well and I'm sure you deliver a powerful word from God. Why wouldn't they pick a young man they can invest in and count on being there for them in the years to come?" He placed his huge hand on my shoulder. "But remember, until you no longer want or need this job, you have to be here on time. Now I'm not angry with you because this is the first time in two years. But don't get lazy on this job as you grow in your others." He removed his hand, stepped back and prepared to leave.

"I promise I won't do that. And if it becomes too much for me, I'll leave and let you find someone else."

"Good enough," he said, then turned and walked away.

The next two weeks seemed to drag on forever. I didn't hear anything from Deacon Brown that first week. I decided to call Reverend Zimmerman.

"I know why you are calling," he said.

"The suspense is killing me," I said.

"I'm sure you'll make it for these next two weeks or however long it takes for them to make a decision. And no I haven't heard anything at all."

"Not even a comment on how well it went?" I asked.

"Not a thing, James," he replied. For some reason I got the feeling that he was enjoying this exchange.

"You haven't heard something bad and just keeping it away from me?"

"No James," he chuckled. "I haven't heard anything bad. And why do you think it would be bad? You are a wonderful young preacher and I know the sermon went well. You need to relax and let God work His will on your behalf."

His words were relaxing. Maybe I was being much too nervous. If God wanted me to have Bethel, it would happen.

"You're right, sir," I said. "If it is meant to be, it will happen."

"Not meant to be, but God's will. Never forget there is a difference."

"Again, you're absolutely right. If it is God's will."

"Please let me know the minute they notify you that they chose you as their pastor," he said.

Once again, his words were comforting. "I most certainly will," I said and we hung up.

I began to doubt that they would hire me. In fact, I had received an invitation to preach in Columbia and thought that I might consider staying in that region even though I preferred the upper part of the state. I began to doubt my ability as a preacher, and also considered the possibility that no church would hire me because of my age, unless it was one out in the country like in Kelton. Maybe I would have to teach for a few years, and wait for the time when age would not be a factor. After three weeks of constantly doubting my ability, I finally received the call.

"We want to offer the pastor's position here at Bethel," Deacon Brown said. "We don't have a great deal of money but can provide you with a decent salary, and of course it will grow as you help the church to grow."

Listening to him I ascended into an ecstatic state of joy. They really did want me to pastor their church. I didn't even consider the question of salary at that moment. I probably would have agreed to preach for nothing. But salary was the frosting on the cake.

"Reverend Sanders, are you there?"

"Yes, definitely yes, I accept," I shouted into the phone.

"I understand that your semester will be over in a few weeks so why don't we make your official start when school is out?"

"No Deacon Brown, I prefer to start this Sunday if you don't have anyone else for the service," I said now with my confidence built back up. "I come home to Union every weekend, so there is no problem with me being there on time for service on Sunday."

"If that's the case, then can you come over to Gaffney on Saturday so you can meet with the deacon board?" Brown suggested. "We need to get to know each other much better. We are anxious to lay out a direction for the church and also determine what it is that we as a team want to accomplish."

"I agree and will be more than happy to meet you on Saturday. Just let me know what time and I'll be there."

"Oh, one other thing, we don't expect any other church to be a priority over Bethel. Is that going to be a problem for you?"

"Not at all. Bethel will be my number one priority," I said knowing exactly what he was alluding to and that was Bethel in Kelton. "My service in Kelton is every other week and in the evening," I continued. "Unfortunately, they are not big enough yet to hire a full time pastor but soon they will be. At that time then I will resign my position there."

"That's the answer I was hoping to hear. I'll see you on Saturday. I'll call later with the exact time. Until then, study hard young man."

"That, I will do."

"What do you think they're going to want to talk about tomorrow?" I asked Malachi as we headed up Highway 251 to Union.

"Some of the deacons are going to be genuinely interested in your approach to the ministry," he said. "Some others are going to be out to get you before you even start."

"I figured that would be the case. Not all of them probably supported me, and they might be out to prove to the others that they made a mistake."

"You know in every Baptist church there is some jealousy and a little envy of the preacher. And especially a young, light skinned, nice looking preacher like you."

I jerked my head in Malachi's direction. He had never been that complimentary to me. It made me feel good to hear it coming from one of my closest friends. But it didn't make me feel good to know that some members could be so petty as to hold my skin color and my age against me. I turned my attention back to the road as a truck was approaching us from the other side.

"What you need to do is remember some of the advice my Dad gave you when you were ordained."

"Yeah I know." I thought back on my last conversation with Reverend A. C. Duncan almost five years ago. His advice was age old tested methods of the ministry. Stay a step ahead of your congregation at all times. And that would be especially important for me, given my age. The one point he stressed more than any other, was to always love all your members, even those who would try to do harm to you. Jesus never preached that it was acceptable behavior to hold grudges, or to try and get even when a member of your church who said negative things about you, or attempt to undercut what you were trying to accomplish. You must stop that member but you cannot do it with anger and malice. You should always do it with a clear understanding that it is imperative the minister be the shepherd of the flock, and at all times maintain control of his church. Reverend Duncan had also advised me to be open with my congregation. My members should know all the church business and nothing off limits to them. "All things open and honest," I remember him saying. My approach to ministry at Bethel Baptist would be built around those wise words of a very wise sage. Because of men like him and Reverend Zimmerman and of course Prof. Sims, I was ready.

12.

In May 1949, two weeks after Easter, I was installed as the pastor at Bethel Baptist Church in Gaffney. I assured the deacons that I was up to the task of conducting all the ministerial responsibilities, and did not need to wait until school ended. Granddad Sanders had always preached to us that we should never make promises that we couldn't keep. So as difficult as it was to study for final exams and also prepare sermons, with God's help I made it through. At one time I had considered going to summer school but now with my new responsibility I dropped that idea. I was determined to spend the entire summer getting to know my deacons and my members much better. Even though I continued to live at home in Union, practically everyday I drove over to Gaffney and spent time at the church. I soon discovered that my selection had not been a unanimous choice, and also that Bethel was in serious financial trouble.

My opposition had to do with two rather trivial concerns. The first one dealt with age. Many of the members believed I was much too young to head up a growing church, and what they really needed was a much more mature person for the job. But others argued that I could grow with the church, and what they wanted were fresh and new ideas. They were impressed that I had trained under Reverend Zimmerman and ordained by Reverend A. C. Duncan. They won out over the others.

The second concern was even more trivial than the first. Some of the members adamantly argued that I was too light skinned a person to be a good Baptist preacher. They believed all good preachers were dark and had more of the natural Baptist qualities, such as singing, preaching in harmonious rhythm and just essentially being a showman. Ultimately, the more rational and sensible members won out over that concern also.

The second major problem I confronted was the financial ineptness of the Deacons. The members of Bethel did not own the church. The mortgage was in the hands of a white man who had allowed them to get way behind in its monthly payment. One Saturday morning the owner asked to meet with me. We sat in my office in the back of the church, and that is when he dropped the bomb on me.

"Reverend Sanders, I'm not sure how much the deacons shared with you, but you got to know that I haven't received a monthly payment in three months."

"What?" I felt a pit in my stomach.

"You heard me right. In three months." He seemed to be enjoying the bad news.

"Why is that and why did you let it go on so long?" I asked as if trying to put the blame on him.

"Trying to be nice, I guess."

"Mr. James, I'm sorry. But I promise that this problem will be resolved immediately."

"It really has to or I'm going to have to foreclose on you all. I don't want to but you leave me no choice. I got to feed my kids too."

"I understand and this will be resolved." I shook his hand and led him out the door.

That same day I called the members of the deacon board and asked that they meet at the church right at five o'clock. They agreed and the battle was on. We sat in the sanctuary and began the discussion.

"Brothers, why was I not informed that the mortgage on the church had not been paid in over three months?" I asked.

"We didn't want to bother you with that right now," Deacon Davenport said. "Don't worry; we'll take care of it."

"But I am worried," I retorted. "There is no reason why this church should ever get three months in the arrears. We have money coming in from various activities. Is all the money consolidated?"

"No, not at all," Deacon Gist, one of the deacons adamantly opposed to my selection, spoke up. "Each auxiliary takes care of its own money."

"Is there one person who knows how much each auxiliary is bringing in?" I asked rather shocked at the disorganization.

"I don't believe so," Deacon Brown chimed in.

"That has to change immediately," I said.

"What do you mean, it has to change?" Deacon Gist shot back.

"Just that, we have to consolidate all the money into one big pot and use it to pay all the bills." I wasn't about to back down.

"Young man, you can't come in here and start making demands insisting that we change the way we have done business at this church for years," Deacon Davenport scowled at me. He had sided with Gist and I began to worry that I might lose this battle.

"You men have hired me to be the head of this church and now you want to put limitations on me. It can't be both ways. Either you want me to lead through the blessings of God or you want to tie my hands at which time I will not be capable of being the pastor that you want and need." This was the first test of my authority and I had to win this battle or I'd never be in control of my church. I knew I was taking a calculated risk putting what could be viewed as an ultimatum to a bunch of men that really didn't know me that well. But it had to be done. My leadership had to be solid and without interference. I wasn't sure if I had won this gamble.

I was relieved when Deacon Brown came to my defense. "Brothers, we have to let our new pastor run his church as he is directed by God," he said looking directly at Deacon Gist. As President of this Deacon Board I suggest that we allow Pastor Sanders to consolidate all financial activities under one umbrella to be controlled by him.

Deacon Gist jumped to his feet and shouted.

"If you do that I will leave this church immediately."

I remained silent, as it was best that I allow this to be played out among the deacons. I had the support of Deacon Brown, and that's all I needed to win this battle.

"How can you let this man come in here and cause this kind of confusion in our church," Deacon Gist continued to shout.

"Because the congregation made it quite clear that he was the man they wanted to see and hear in the pulpit every Sunday. We are the servants of the people and they have spoken," Deacon Brown retorted.

"If you do this I will leave this church," Deacon Gist said in a calmer tone.

"Then this Deacon Board is willing to accept your resignation tonight, and I then move that we adopt our pastor's suggestion immediately."

Deacon Jordan who seldom said much jumped to his feet.

"I second that we accept Deacon Gist's resignation and move to adopt the changes suggested by our pastor."

"How do you vote brothers?" Deacon Brown asked.

Eight of the ten Deacons voted in the affirmative. Deacon Davenport voted with Gist but was not willing to follow him out of the church.

"I'm sure that you all will live to regret this vote," Deacon Gist scowled. "May God help you to see the error in your ways." He then turned and stomped down the aisle and out of the church.

I had won the first confrontation and established myself as the head of my flock. Now I had to make sure that Gist's prediction would never come true.

After that initial challenge to my authority, the Deacon Board and I began meeting every Saturday morning to lay out long term plans for Bethel. We agreed that it had room for growth, and that we had to reach out to the non- church going members of our community and win them over to Bethel. We also agreed that a strong youth program and Sunday school was an essential ingredient for a church on the move. The children would be the eventual members in the future, and along with recruiting people from the community I was convinced that Bethel would become a flagship church in Gaffney. I was also determined that no preacher in the entire city and for that matter in the state of South Carolina would ever out preach me. Bethel deserved the right to brag that they had the best minister in all the state.

The one question the mothers of the church repeatedly asked me all the time was when did I plan to marry? Specifically, when would I find a fine young lady at Bethel and get married. They raised the issue so often that I finally got the message. They did not want a pastor without a first lady.

One Sunday in the fall of 1949 I met that one person who I knew would be my wife. Problem was she did not attend Bethel but instead Limestone Baptist Church on the other side of town. I recall that special day when I met Rubye Corry. I noticed her when she strolled into the church and found a seat up front next to Annie Louis one of my members who constantly bragged that she had a perfect young lady for me. She sat tall and proper just like she owned the place. The black dress, red shoes, and red hat contrasted perfectly with her beautiful peach skin color. She sat next to a couple other girls and stared up at me as if to say, "yes I'm here so get ready." I just knew that our eyes locked in on each other and she fully understood there could be only one outcome from this first meeting.

I quickly looked away from her and at Annie. I was used to folks always trying to introduce me to their sisters, aunts, daughters and friends. To be honest, most of the time the women never measured up but not this time. Annie winked at me as if to say "I told you so." I arched my eyebrows as a gesture that she was right.

After church service was over, I stood in my usual place in the front entrance shaking hands as the congregation filed out. A new kind of excitement surged through my body as I shook hands but watched closely for that pretty lady in the red hat and black dress. Finally I spotted her standing in the line right behind Annie, waiting her turn to shake my hand. I had this one opportunity to establish something more than a handshake with her.

When Sister Esther Boyle grabbed my hand, I knew it would be a struggle to free myself from her grip. Every Sunday, she would stand in that line and wait her turn to be close to me. Usually, I was willing to tolerate her obvious advances, but not this time. Despite my attempts to wrench my hand from hers I failed. Each time I tried to free myself, her grip tightened. You could tell that she had spent many a day and night out in the fields. Her hands were rough and her grip very tight.

"Reverend Sanders, you preach better and better every week," she said while clutching to my hand.

"God bless you, Sister Boyle," I said, still trying to free my hand. I glanced at the line and saw the young lady in the black dress getting real close to me. I felt relieved because she didn't just give up. "You have a good day, Sister Boyle, and remember Jesus loves you," I said hoping that she would get the hint and move on.

"Now if you need a good meal this afternoon just come on over to the house," she said still holding my hand. She squeezed so tight I thought she might cut off my circulation. "I got a side of beef, potato salad, greens, corn bread and fresh okra. You got to eat real good so you can keep on bringing the word of God to us."

Every living person in Gaffney knew just how much I loved to eat. In fact there was a joke told about me that every time I came into town, the rooster gathered up all the hens and headed for the hills until I was gone. Fried chicken was my favorite. I was surprised when Sister Boyle teased me with a side of beef and not fried chicken.

"Thank you Sister Boyle but I have to get on back to Union cause I have to preach a sermon for Reverend Zimmerman this afternoon." The lady in the black dress was only a couple people behind Sister Boyle as others had given up and went around her. They knew it would be a while before she relinquished her position right in front of me.

Finally Sister Boyle decided to move on but not before she finished with a few words about my status.

"You know Pastor Sanders the church folk been talking about you still being a single man," she said as she finally gave me back my right hand. "Plenty of fine young ladies in this church, and anyone of them would make you a fine wife. You better think on that and do something real soon." She finished and moved away leaving Annie standing right in front of me.

I smiled and said, "Thanks for bringing a guest."

Annie smiled back and then stepped aside. I stood face to face with the beautiful young lady, and gave her my best flirtatious smile.

"A real fine service Pastor," she said as she extended her hand to me and I grasped it.

"Thank you," I said. "My sermons come right from the Lord. I am just the messenger delivering His message." I placed my free hand on top of hers and held it in a warm grip. "May I ask your name and what church do you attend?"

"Rubye Corry and I'm a member at Limestone Baptist Church, here in Gaffney," she said.

"What brings you over to Bethel?" I asked in a rather rhetorical manner. I know darn well why she was there. All the young girls were attending Bethel just to see who this new, young preacher was.

"Gaffney is not a real big town and when one of the few churches gets a new preacher, it is not unusual to visit and hear him preach," she said. " Annie invited me and my two girlfriends to come hear you today." She pointed to two young ladies who were standing off to the side talking to some of the ladies that belonged to Bethel.

"You live here in Gaffney?" I asked. Unlike Sister Boyle I did not want to release her hand and definitely wanted to know a lot more about her.

"Yes, when I'm not away to school."

"You're a college student?"

"Yes indeed. I attend North Carolina A and T. I'll be leaving in a couple of weeks to start summer school."

She was leaving to go back to school. That meant I had to increase the level of interrogation. I had to know exactly who this beautiful lady was, and most important if I possibly could see her outside of the church. I knew that meant meeting and talking to her parents. I'd have to get their permission to see her but I also knew that would be no problem. Most parents were delighted when an eligible preacher showed interest in their daughter. But first, I had to get her interested in me.

"I know a beautiful young lady such as yourself probably is already spoken for and there is a boy in your life?"

"Yes there is," she said and that practically knocked me off my feet. "I've had the same boyfriend since high school, and we'll probably get married."

That knocked me even further backward. I had to figure a way to get around this hindrance.

"Well, he certainly is a lucky young man. You must bring him to the church sometime. In fact you should consider changing churches and moving over here to Bethel. We are the growing church and I'm determined soon we'll be the biggest and best church in Gaffney."

Rubye pulled her hand away from my grip and stepped back from me. "Thank you Pastor, but I'm perfectly happy at Limestone."

"But don't forget us over here and if you ever want to visit again, I'll make sure you are my special guest."

"Thank you Pastor," she said and smiled. "I'll keep that in mind. But I have to go now. You preached a mighty fine sermon and I'll let my friends know they should at least come here and hear you at least one time. But no one from Limestone will be changing churches."

I realized that I had put my foot in my mouth. The last thing I wanted was to compete with Prof. Sims. He was my mentor, my teacher and I wanted Bethel to grow with Limestone, not compete against it. I felt bad.

I watched as Rubye strolled back over to where her friends were waiting. I knew that if she turned and looked back there was some interest on her part. Just as I expected, when she reached her friends, she looked back and smiled. I smiled back and then turned to shake the hand of another young lady who waited patiently for me to stop flirting with this beautiful young lady in the black dress.

Every Sunday for the next three months I anxiously stared at the front door to the church while the choir sang and the collection was taken in anticipation of her walking back into Bethel. But she never did come back. I asked around the town about her and even had the opportunity to discuss her with the pastor at Limestone. To my disappointment the report was always the same. She was in a very serious relationship, and her parents had given the young man permission to take her out without a chaperone. That was serious business in the south. Black parents were very protective of their daughters.

The young girls from proper church going families never went out alone, especially after dark. That attitude was a carry over from years of abuse by a racist society. Many of the white men in the South felt it was their right to attack and rape Black girls. Their thinking was based on the false assumption that all Black women sought the company of white men, and nothing could be further from the truth. Not only did Black parents believe they had to protect their daughters from the attacks by white men but also they had to protect them from over aggressive Black boys. When informed that Rubye was now able to go out with her boyfriend at night without being accompanied by another person, I knew my chances of getting to know her better were slim. I turned my attention back to other young women but found no one that matched the girl in the black dress.

The summer seemed to fly by. I guess that was because I was so busy building up Bethel in Gaffney and still preaching at the other Bethel in Kelton. I had no spare time at all and that's what I preferred. All my life I had good role models who set an outstanding example as to what the man was expected to do in society, and the most important responsibility was to work. But as the summer drew to a close I had to re-direct my energy back to Benedict, and completing my education.

13.

My heartbeat quickened and my breathing was heavy as I watched her walk through the front entrance to the church, down the center aisle, and find a seat five pews back from the front. It had been a very long time since I first met the lady in the black and red. I assumed she'd married the young man she seemed so committed to back when I talked with her, right outside the church. My initial excitement waned when I recalled her words to me. She was involved in a serious relationship and very happy with the young man whom she planned to marry once she graduated from college. But now she was back at my church and obviously had come to hear me preach. At least I knew she considered me a preacher worth coming back to hear deliver a sermon. I need not read anymore into it, because no doubt she was still involved in her relationship. She was with the same two young ladies that had accompanied her the first time she came here. I needed to pray.

Quietly I prayed, "Lord do not let this lady enter my thoughts to the point that I cannot deliver my message for you today."

"In order not to concentrate on her, look out into the congregation and never look directly at her," were the words I received from the Lord.

"Thank you Lord," I said in a low whisper. "But I think that's going to be easier said than done."

While waiting my turn to deliver the sermon I looked everywhere in the church except at her. But I could feel her eyes on me or maybe it was my imagination; or maybe wishful thinking.

I definitely wanted her to glance at me often. We never did make eye contact. Every time I stared out into the congregation and my eyes fell on her, she was looking elsewhere. Why was she here and why did she want to torment me this way? Finally it was my turn to preach.

I had never felt so nervous delivering a message from God since my first sermon for ordination and I knew she was to blame. But I also had never felt so inspired than at that very moment. I wanted to impress her and that was not good. The only person that I should want to impress was God. But maybe He would understand and not be upset with my one time allowing vanity and ego to enter into my pulpit.

I was good that day, and proof of my effectiveness was the seven new members who came forward to join Bethel. She was not one of the seven, but I still felt good about my success on that Sunday. The irony was that I preached on how through prayer God provides you with all you need in life for happiness. I felt in my spirit that she was all I needed for happiness, but the problem was that I didn't dare pray for the breakup of another relationship in order for my desires to be fulfilled.

When the service finally ended I hurried back to the door in order to greet the congregation that wanted to have words with me. As members filed by, shook my hand and congratulated me for a fine sermon I kept looking to see if she was in line. I sighed as I saw her standing in the line. After at least twenty members had filed by she stood there right in front of me.

We politely shook hands and I said.

"It's Miss Rubye Corry isn't it?" I purposely said Miss.

"I see you have an excellent memory," she said. "Yes you have the name correct."

"Welcome back to Bethel," I said. "I'm so pleased to see you again."

"Your sermon was quite good today," she said.

"Thank God because it's all Him. I'm just a vessel used to preach His word. Have you graduated from college yet?" I asked

"I graduated last month. I'll be teaching here in Gaffney."

With great reluctance for fear of her answer I asked. "How is the young man I believe you were seeing when I last talked with you?"

A somber expression spread across her face. She was not smiling at all. For a moment I feared I had asked the wrong question, maybe probed too much into her private life. I needed to change the subject.

"He passed away unexpectedly last year."

"Ms. Corry, I'm so sorry," I said. "Was he ill?"

"Yes, suddenly he became ill and they weren't able to save him."

"Please accept my condolences but also you must know that God does all things for a reason. And that your friend is already at a place we all hope to go someday."

"I know and that is what has given me the strength to carry on. I did love him and miss him so much. But I know I must get on with my life."

"As we all must do when we lose a loved one."

"Thank your Reverend. I appreciate your words."

I reached out and took her hand.

"Please feel free to visit us here at Bethel any time, and if there is anything that I can do for you during your time of mourning don't hesitate to call on me."

"I'll remember that." She ended our conversation, pulled her hand away from me and walked to meet her friends. This time she did not look back.

After I shook the last hand, I hurried back into the church and to my office. I needed to sit alone and pray. How could I possibly pursue this lady I admired so much, given what she had gone through. I didn't want it to appear that I was taking advantage of another person's tragedy. But I still knew that she was the lady who had to be my wife. There was no question about it. The only question was how long I had to wait before I felt comfortable asking her to begin a relationship with me, and how long did she also feel she had to wait before accepting my advances.

It took exactly a month before Rubye finally decided to invite me over to talk with her parents about the possibility of the two of us going out together. Nathaniel Corry, Rubye's father worked for the Department of Public Works in Gaffney, which at that time, was quite a good job. Bessie Corry did domestic work for different families around town. Mrs. Bessie was a very strong and dominant mother who scrutinized the boys that wanted to date her two daughters. She never allowed them to go out without a chaperone, at least not for the first dozen dates. And any man, regardless of his status or position in life, had to seek permission from Mrs. Bessie in order to date her daughters. Rubye's father was much more relaxed, very quiet and reserved. Her mother made all decisions about Rubye. Even though they did not attend Bethel, I knew that my greatest advantage was that most mothers approved of their daughters taking up with an established pastor, and especially one who was also a college graduate. I knew that when I met with them one Sunday afternoon after church. Mrs. Bessie had invited me over for dinner.

The afternoon was off to a great start when she served baked chicken. The entire city knew how much I loved chicken because it was considered somewhat of a delicacy. She also served rice, greens, okra, corn bread, fresh squeezed lemonade, and topped it off with peach cobbler. After dinner we retired to the living room and got down to the subject at hand.

"Rubye thinks she might be interested in going out with you in a social setting," Mrs. Bessie began the discussion.

"Yes ma'am," I said.

"Let me assure you, young man, that I am not interested in my daughter going out with a philandering preacher man. Do you understand?" She scowled.

Her comment caught me off guard. I didn't resent it because I would agree that a young lady as beautiful and precious as Ruby, should not get trapped into a relationship going no where. Also, my interest in Rubye was deep and would be lasting.

"I absolutely understand and agree with you," I said. "I can assure you that I am not a philandering preacher, and my intentions toward your daughter are honorable."

I couldn't help but notice that Mr. Corry was reared back in his big recliner with a serious expression all over his face. He wasn't saying anything but was doing his own assessment of me. No doubt he analyzed everything I said and would share his opinion later with his wife. Rubye sat quite rigid with legs crossed and arms folded, waiting patiently for the outcome. This exchange was limited to Mrs. Bessie and me.

"Rubye isn't a member of Bethel but is dedicated to her church at Limestone," Mrs. Bessie said. "If you start dating a girl that is not a member of your church, how do you think all the available young girls at Bethel going to feel?"

"They probably won't be too happy, but I have to go with my feelings and where the Lord leads me. Right now He is telling me that Rubye is the right person for me. I don't plan to go against the will of God. He's brought me this far at a very young age, and I know He'll never lead me astray."

A smile spread across Mrs. Bessie's face and I instantly knew that she liked my response. What she didn't know is that I was not trying to impress her with those words, but sincerely meant that I only had to please God. I still liked the fact that she appreciated my explanation.

"I understand that your parents live over in Union," she said.

At that point I knew the decision had been made and she was making small talk. She already knew they lived there.

"Yes ma'am," I said. "I was born and raised there. Only time I been away are the two years at Benedict"

"You plan to keep on living there?" She asked with some substance now. She was assessing her daughter's possible future, and would she be leaving Gaffney.

"No ma'am, I will go where the Lord calls me. Right now He has called me to do His work here in Gaffney and the church is going to build me a home right next door. It should be complete within the next two years."

Again, that smile.

"I guess it will be all right for Rubye to see you in a social setting," Mrs. Bessie said. "But I am sure you know the rules. There must always be a chaperone with you and my daughter does not stay out after ten o'clock."

"I understand and that is perfectly acceptable to me."

With Mrs. Bessie's approval, I began to see Rubye on a regular basis along with the chaperone. We usually attended church functions and once in a while we went to a movie. One weekend after we had been dating for a couple months, we drove to Union and I introduced her to Mama and Poppa. They instantly took to her and I believe Mama knew that I would one day marry Rubye. How she knew, I'm not sure. I guess it was that motherly instinct.

On the final Saturday before I had to return to Benedict for the fall semester, I drove to Gaffney, picked up Rubye and a friend and drove again to Union, this time to introduce her to my best friend, Malachi. Later he told me the same thing as Mama, that she would someday be my wife. I knew it, my best friend knew it, and Mama did also. It was meant to be, but first I had to get through my last two years at Benedict.

In the fall 1950, Latta transferred over to Benedict and was assigned to the same dorm as Malachi and me. The three of us were a strong representation for the small country town of Union. The majority of our classes were in the Starks School of Religion. The most useful one was the class on Homiletics taught by Dr. Brown. I adopted many of the preaching techniques we covered from the classroom into the real world at Bethel.

During that fall semester I stayed extremely busy. Between my responsibilities at the church, my studies and squeezing some time in to be with Rubye, I sometimes felt that I was in over my head. But I had no choice in the matter. There was no way I would give up school or the church and definitely was not about to give up the love of my life. However, I did give up any kind of activities at the school. One of those activities was my job lighting the fire every morning.

"James, James, you got to get up," Malachi said as he nudged me out of an enjoyable sleep. "It's after five and they going to be awfully upset if you don't get over to the cafeteria and get that fired started."

"I'm not going," I mumbled. "I'm tired, it's awfully cold and

I just can't do all these things any more." I buried my head deep in my pillow.

"You got to go or can't nobody eat."

"Reverend Bailey can start the fire."

"What if he isn't there?"

"He'll be. Leave me alone. I want to sleep."

Malachi continued. "You going to quit?" He asked.

"Guess so, cause I'm sure not going this morning."

"Dean Riley going to be all over you for this. You know how much he stresses responsibility."

I rose half way up in the bed while keeping the covers pulled up to my neck and covering my shoulders.

"I can't do this any more, Dunc. We've been making this trip back and forth from Union to Bennett for over three years. All that time we been preaching and studying and practically have no life of our own." I paused to yawn. "I don't mind the studying so much and you know I love the preaching but getting up at five o'clock to start a fire so others can eat is gotten to be a little too much to handle."

"So you going to just leave them like this?"

"Don't worry Dunc, old Reverend will be there to get it started. He trusted me a lot but not to the point that he wouldn't be there in the morning. Can you believe in all these years he's never missed a day. He got to have a lot of vacation time built up."

"I'm going over there." Malachi moved back away from my bed and slipped into his clothes and shoes. "I'll let them know you're not coming and I guess you all will deal with the repercussions later." Duncan finished and headed out of the room.

I lay back down and pulled the covers up over my head. I wasn't sure what those repercussions would be, but at that particular moment I really didn't care. I was tired and planned to rest before classes the next day on Tuesday. I had lit my last fire. I did that for over two years, and now it was time to allow some other deserving student to make that money toward tuition. I was set with my salary from the church.

There were many times I would have preferred to remain on campus for the weekend because of some of the activities the ministerial students were involved in. One of those events occurred right before Christmas break. Malachi and I were not there but Latta told us about it.

Right before the Christmas break in 1950, a contingent of divinity students from Clemson University showed up at our campus. Dean Riley contacted the ministerial students on campus that weekend and introduced them to the Clemson students. Latta was one of those students. They spent hours talking about every subject from Moses and the Jews oppression in Egypt to the similarities between them and the Blacks in the South. Dean Riley invited them to have lunch; they accepted and were treated to some good old soul food cooking. It was a great afternoon and they invited us to visit their campus and attend Chapel service.

Dean Riley and a group of our students made the trip to Clemson on a Sunday morning. Again I couldn't go nor could Malachi because of our obligations. Latta did go and the Benedict students actually taught Sunday school classes at the Clemson Chapel, attended the morning service and were served lunch by the Clemson students. As our students prepared to leave Dr. Riley asked Reverend Allen, who was the pastor at the Clemson Chapel and advisor to the Clemson students, would there be any repercussions for allowing our students to attend service in what was a segregated church? His response was rather prophetic.

" If repercussions come" he said, "they just have to come. I'm persuaded that in the years to come the most popular place for the clergy will be jail."

That year the Sanders' family had one of their best Christmas's ever. Nette had graduated from West Virginia State University and taken a teaching job somewhere near Washington, D.C., but had come home for the holidays. Grady had joined the army and was home for the holidays, so we all were home to celebrate with Mama and Poppa.

After opening all our presents we went next door to Grandpa Sanders for breakfast. It was a tradition of the family. We then went to Corinth for an early Christmas service. And after that I was off to Gaffney to have a special Christmas service at Bethel and dinner with Rubye and her family. I could tell that Mama wasn't real happy about that because she was slowly losing her oldest son to the woman he would eventually marry. As a matter of fact I felt a little uneasy. I had dated but never so serious that I spent Christmas with someone else.

When I arrived home that evening, I gave Mama special attention and when I did she smiled as if to say it's okay son because I knew this day would eventually come. And as much as I enjoyed Jesus' birthday that year, I enjoyed the New Year's Eve festivities just as much. It would be my first watch service at Bethel and that made it special. Churches throughout the south celebrated watch service on New Years Eve. The primary reason this was such a special occasion is because it was our opportunity to pay homage and respect to our ancestors, who in the year 1862 sat in their small churches throughout the south, and waited for the clock to strike midnight.

The New Year ushered a new beginning for our ancestors, who had been locked in the terrible vice of slavery because it was the exact time that the Emancipation Proclamation went into effect. It freed all slaves held in the Confederate states. And even though they recognized the difficulty making it in a free world without resources they were determined to be free. So on that night for the past eighty-eight years watch services had been conducted upholding a tradition within the Black culture. And determined to up-hold that practice Bethel had a packed house and we stayed in service from ten until after one o'clock with old time testimony, singing and even a little dancing. In the end we all pledged to get closer to God and to do Jesus' work here on earth as He was doing our work with our Father in Heaven. After the service we returned to Mama and Poppa's house, toasted with some Apple Cider, then we all went to bed. The next day I was up early, on my way back to Benedict.

< The Spiritual Journey of a Legend >

14.

The fall semester of 1951 was rather uneventful and I was so busy preaching at two different churches and taking classes in the school of religion that days and weeks seemed to fly by.

Our most excitement happened when Dean Riley summoned all the ministerial students to a conference in his office. We knew it had to be something of a very serious nature because the meeting was called on the spur of the moment, and it involved all of us. We met in the college's large conference room next to the president's office. Dean Riley got right to the point.

"Over the past month, there have been a number of suspicious fires in Osborne Hall, the girl's dormitory. These fires haven't done a great deal of damage because we were able to put them out rather quickly. But it has caused some panic among our young ladies." He paused to allow us to take in what he was telling us. "Many of the girls believe we have a serial arsonist among us. Don't worry; I didn't call this meeting because we believe it was one of you all."

All twenty-two of us sighed and looked at each other as if to say "thank God."

"We believe it is someone off the campus, and we know we'll eventually catch him."

"When you do, let us have hold of him," one of the students called out from his position standing in the back of the room.

"Now that is not the kind of spirit we want to hear from

our future preachers. Remember the primary foundation of Christianity is forgiveness," he retorted to the student's comment and then continued. "Many of our girls are frightened and in fact have called their parents to come and get them. They want to leave the campus because they do not believe it is safe."

"How can we help?" One of the students asked.

"By giving the girls your rooms and you move into Osborne Hall, at least until we catch the person causing the harm."

"Is there enough room for us?" A student asked.

"Yes, we've already figured out the sleeping arrangements," Dean Riley quickly answered.

Since they had already figured it out, it didn't seem that we had much of a choice, I thought. But it was nice of him to ask.

"When do you want us to move?" I finally asked.

"Immediately, like first thing in the morning."

"What about our classes?" Malachi asked.

"We'll arrange it with your Professors. Most of you are taking religious courses tomorrow so it'll be easy to make provisions to miss that one day and make it up at a later time."

"Just think fellows, we can put this on our resume when we look for work," another student said jokingly. "What is any nobler than to give up your comfortable home and move into a place that is under attack from some maniac, and all for the cause of the opposite sex?"

"Hail to the opposite sex," we all chanted. "Hail to the opposite sex."

"Thank you men," Dean Riley interrupted our fun. "I'm sure the young ladies, the president, and the trustees will thank you also in the future. But let's get this done by tomorrow. You all are dismissed."

We spent most of the next day helping the girls move their belongings from Osborne Hall into our dorm right across Oak Street. Then we moved our belongings into their dorm. Malachi and I were assigned a room on the second floor away from where most of the damage on the first floor. Latta got stuck on the first floor.

We would never move back to our old dorm. Julia Starks, the widow of the first Black president at Benedict promised us that she would find new and better lodging for us and she did just that. She convinced a white family that owned a large white mansion right next to the campus on Hardin Boulevard to sell their property to the school. How she managed to convince them to sell was the talk of the campus for a long time. However she did it, she was successful and we finished our final year at Benedict in our new housing accommodations.

There was something very special about the spring semester of 1952. It was the beginning of my last semester at Benedict. In just five months I would be a college graduate and hopefully a full time teacher at a school somewhere around Gaffney because, even though I had to teach, my first love was my ministry and pastor's position at Bethel. During my last semester I stressed three important goals, the first was to pass all courses so I would be able to graduate, the second was to begin to look for teaching positions, and the third was to prepare for the graduation ceremony in May.

The second week we returned to school from Christmas break, the seniors had a meeting to organize for our graduation. One of the items on the agenda was publication of the Yearbook. Malachi and I were assigned to the Advertising Committee. Our job was to go out into the community and solicit funds from businesses that were inclined to take out an ad space in the book. I didn't particularly like that assignment but did my best to help raise the funds. We must have visited every Black business and most of the white businesses in Columbia. Most of our ads came from the Blacks, but I was pleased at the number of whites who were willing to support our effort. It dawned on me that most of them were located in the Black community and depended on our people for their business. That probably gave them some kind of bragging rights with their customers.

Malachi and I were successful and raised enough money to support the publication of the yearbook. For that reason we enjoyed hero status for at least a couple of weeks. Every student was assigned a day and time to get his or her picture taken by the local Black photographer. It took a couple of weeks to complete the picture taking and placing of the ads in the right spot in the yearbook. But by the beginning of April we had a finished product and I have to admit that we had a great looking yearbook. We did this and still managed to maintain our grades, go home on the weekends, and in my case, preach every Sunday at two different churches.

On Saturday, May 27, the entire graduating class of fifty-two students proudly marched into Kirkland Chapel where the graduation ceremony would take place. The guest speaker for the graduation was Dr. W. W. Long, from Atlanta, Georgia. We took our seats behind him up on the stage. A number of local dignitaries spoke first, there were a couple of gospel songs by Antioch Baptist Church of Columbia, and then President Bacoates stepped up to the podium and introduced the speaker.

Dr. Long spoke for a half hour. He congratulated the class for our accomplishment. We were, according to him that talented tenth of the population that had earned a degree but our accomplishments could not end there. The degree was just the beginning, and by accepting the respect of our community we had to accept the responsibility also. He then read a passage from the "Old Testament." Samson had slain the lion and after some time when he returned bees had made honey in the lion's head. He then told us that we must first slay our fears and once we do that we can begin to accomplish whatever we set out to do.

He also told us that this country would soon begin to change and, we, the new generation of Black leaders, would be in the forefront of that change. It would not be easy and we would confront many obstacles but through God, prayer and sheer will power we would prevail. His final words were to never lose faith, love one another as Jesus loved us, take up the mantle for an improved world, and march forward into the second decade of the Twentieth Century.

With those final words, Dr. Long sat back down and Dr. Bacoates presented each of us with our degree. After he called the final student's name, we stood and tossed our graduation caps in the air, indicating that we were about to take on the challenges that Dr. Long articulated to us as college graduates, teachers, and as preachers.

15.

There is a long period of silence. I look up from my recorder and notice that Reverend Sanders' eyes are closed and his breathing seems rather heavy. But just as if he knew I was looking at him, he opens his eyes.

"Are you all right?" I ask.

"Yes, just fine," he answers. "Whenever I close my eyes, visions of those years come rushing back to me," he continues. "That Saturday afternoon when we received our degrees seemed to change all of us. And the change was based on the challenge presented to us by Dr. Long."

"How did it change you?" I ask.

"Turn off the recorder and let's just chat for a few minutes," he instructs.

I comply and click the off button. I then move in just a little closer to him. I perceive him to be a man of extreme wisdom and knowledge. Much of who we are as a Black race and culture emanates from men like Dr. Sanders. I feel that he wants to affect my thinking in the same manner that Prof. Sims and Reverend Zimmerman, as well as his father and grandfather affected him. He recognizes the importance of passing on his experience in dealing with a racist society for a great deal of his life, to others so that we never will allow that to happen to our race and people again. Reverend Sanders, Reverend Duncan, and Dr. Latta Thomas hold the key to unlock what is great about our race.

I feel a chill pass through my body as I recognize that soon we will lose these great men, and my generation must be prepared to carry on the legacy that they have established for us. He finally continues.

"Those years after graduating from Benedict were the best and worst of times. They were the best because we perfected the ability to live under the veil." He pauses to assess my response.

I have none simply because I am not sure where he is going with this line of thinking.

"The idea of the veil as articulated by Dr. Du Bois was very clear to all of us. It was a West African tradition that all children are born with a veil-like membrane covering its head and it creates special spiritual powers and strengths. Those powers brought out the best in us and helped in our survival. However, outside that veil was an ugly world that we were forced to deal with every day, but on Sunday. It consisted of people who felt that their skin color made them superior, and nothing can be more foolish than the notion that something as superficial as color makes someone superior to another. That was the worst. Do you understand where I'm going with this line of thinking?"

"I'm not sure," I answer.

"Sunday was the one day that we didn't have to deal outside the veil. Sunday was the day that we could be ourselves, expressing love for each other, nurture our children, and talk about a better world for Black people, and it all took place in the church."

"I think I understand now. The church again had to carry the burden of the race in freedom as it did during slavery."

"Exactly, and it fell on the shoulders of men like Malachi, Latta and me. We had to be the shoulder for the entire race to cry on after they endured unbelievable suffering during the week. And why? Simply because insecure people needed someone to feel they were better than in order to feed their insecurity. But in the long run it made us a tougher, stronger, and a more loving people having endured all the violence and ugliness of an apartheid system."

He extends his hand for me to take. I reach out and clasp mine into his and he holds it tightly.

"The great Black theologian, Howard Thurman once said

the measure of a man's estimate of your strength is the kind of weapons he feels that he must use in order to hold you fast in a prescribed place. I memorized that saying and thought of it every time I read of another lynching, the stealing of a Black man's property, the rape of our woman and any other atrocious acts that were committed against us during those terrible years. When you pair his sayings with the inordinate amount of weapons they used to keep us down, then you feel proud knowing that your strength comes from God, and try as they did they could never break us down."

Reverend Sanders finishes and closes his eyes for a moment. It gives me time to reflect on my own relationship to this man, and to others like him in the Palmetto state. I think of Congressman James Clyburn, who has followed in the footsteps of other great Congressmen from South Carolina like my distant relative, Joseph H. Rainey. I smile and conclude that there is no place quite like South Carolina and even though I no longer live here it will always remain my home. From the tobacco city of Mullins which hosts the Golden Leaf festival to the Chitterling Strut in Salley, to the huge peach that symbolizes the Peach city of Gaffney, and to the thriving city of Columbia and the coastal city of Myrtle Beach, there just is no place like my home state.

Reverend Sanders finally opens his eyes, and says. "Let's continue. We are quickly running out of time.

16.

Rubye Corry, soon to be Sanders, looked absolutely beautiful as she strolled down the center aisle of Bethel Baptist Church on July 24, 1952. I stood in the front of the church next to my best man, Malachi, and watched Mr. Corry escort Rubye to my side to become my wife. Reverend A. C. Duncan stood in front of us with a Bible in his hand, prepared to join the two of us as man and wife.

The church was packed, as I believe every member of Bethel and Limestone was there for this momentous occasion. The young, handsome bachelor minister was about to take a wife and give Bethel a stunningly gorgeous first lady. People were standing in the vestibule trying to get in, or at least look inside as the ceremony was going on. The church was actually so crowded Rubye had trouble getting into the sanctuary and down the aisle. But at a little past two o'clock we became man and wife.

At the reception, we must have stood in the receiving line for two hours, and then another two for the picture taking and the dinner. Finally we changed clothes and left on our drive to New Jersey for a week long honeymoon. On the way up there, Rubye made the comment that I might lose half my females due to jealousy. Many of my members at Bethel were upset because I was marrying someone outside the church. Some of the women actually threatened to quit Bethel.

I said if that happened then it was the desire of the Lord and I would just have to go out and find new members. We were married and that was the way the Lord wanted it. We had fulfilled his dictate to us and that was all we could do.

Two weeks later when we returned to Gaffney, I felt good as I prepared for service that first Sunday. But Rubye and I were shocked to find the sanctuary half empty. Evidently many of the female members had decided to boycott because I had married her. I called it more like pouting. Rubye felt guilty that it was her fault, but I quickly dispelled those thoughts assuring her that I did what was right for me and for her, and that is all that matters. I reminded her that I had promised to go out and find all new members if the others stayed away.

Rubye had also saved up some money as a teacher. When she told me about the savings I insisted that she give it to her parents. I was not about to allow my wife to take on any responsibility for the financial security of my family. If I used her money to get us started, I would always feel guilty. She reluctantly gave her parents the money, and I do believe that my actions were well respected by her parents, and I believe by her also.

Rubye and I did not live together the first year of our marriage. It would take that long for the church to finish the parsonage. I stayed in Union with Mama and Poppa while she continued to live with her parents. In the fall of 1952, I was hired as the principal and teacher in Lukesville, South Carolina, a mill town twenty miles from Union. The Blacks who lived in the town worked on the grounds outside the mill doing menial work, and some drove trucks from the mill to the warehouse where the cotton was stored until shipped out. Unlike the whites, they were not allowed to work inside the mill where the better paying jobs were located. In fact, they couldn't even go inside unless there was an emergency, and then a white worker accompanied them.

Other Blacks worked as sharecroppers for the white plantation owners. Most of the Blacks could not read or write, and the children were allowed to attend school for a few months out of the year due to their parents' need to have them working in the fields. Life was rough in Lukesville and teaching was just as rough.

Lukesville Elementary School had two teachers, a lady who had to be in her late forties with only a high school diploma and me. I served as the Principal since I had the college degree. The building was an old abandoned house with two rooms. It had been fixed up by the parents but still was lacking in most amenities conducive for a decent learning environment. I taught grades three through six. I felt nothing but compassion for those poor children. Many of their parents did not understand the importance of education. They only understood the urgency of their children working to help to pay off their yearly debt.

As teachers, we were required to do all things from teaching to lighting the fire in the fireplace in order to keep the old raggedy wooden building warm. We also had to repair holes in the walls and leaks in the roof. We had to deal with illnesses that occurred quite often, children sleeping in class, and short tempers along with the fights that accompanied those tempers. After all that, we had to teach.

Worst of all was watching young minds come into the classroom with a burning desire to learn. They wanted to spell, read and do math just as any young child desires. But there were so many obstacles in their way, learning became impossible. Billy Hamilton was one of those special students. He was always on time in the morning, and would often stay after school to help me out. He always sought information about school, and I knew the reason why. He wanted to escape the drudgery of his life. One day after school he opened up to me.

"Mr. Sanders how did you get to go to college?" he asked.

"First I had to graduate from high school, and then I had to apply to college and get accepted," I answered.

"I wish I could go to the same college you went to someday, and then I'd be as smart as you."

"Billy, you will be able to go to college someday if you study hard and get good grades in high school after you leave here."

"I ain't gonna be able to go to no college. Daddy done tole me I got to work with him when I finish school here."

"Why did he tell you that?" I asked but really knew the answer.

"Cause he got to pay so much to stay on the land he works. You know it don't belong to us. It belongs to the white man, and he real mean if Daddy don't pay him on time."

"What does your Daddy have you do?"

"He make me push the mule with the plow. Sometime he have

me and my sister pull weeds. She don't like doin' it cause of all the snakes. I ain't afraid of no snakes. One time a snake get nasty with her and I jest went over there and cut his head off." A smile spread across Billy's face.

"That's real good because you always have to protect your sister."

"You think you can talk my Daddy into letting me go to high school, then I can go on to college?"

"Yes, Billy, at the right time I will talk to him and let him know that by the time you grow up, college will be necessary to get a decent job."

"Thank you, Mr. Sanders." Billy grabbed his bag and headed to the door. "Can you do it today when he picks me up?"

"No, I can't do it today, but I promise you that I will do it."

He turned and bolted out the door to meet his father.

I never did get a chance to have that talk with Billy's father because he never came to the school to talk about Billy's progress whenever I had a day to meet with the parents. In fact, very few of the parents ever showed up. Even when we gave them sufficient notice they still failed to come. The one day I did go out to Billy's farmhouse to talk with his parents, his daddy never showed up and I only had about ten minutes with his mother. I felt a cold distance between us like she was afraid to talk with me. We talked for about ten minutes and then she excused herself. We never discussed Billy going to college

Every Friday I drove to Gaffney, picked up Rubye and she stayed in Union until Sunday morning when we returned to Gaffney for service at Bethel. Some of the women still resented her, and it showed in their attitudes on Wednesday evening at prayer service, and on Sunday for church service.

Word soon got back to me that people were talking because Rubye and I weren't living together. They wondered why my new wife wouldn't come and live in Union, and they further suspected that I might be messing around and had someone else right there in Union. That rumor practically got out of control when I loaned my car to Grady one night, not knowing he planned to spend some time at a location known as a hangout for lovers.

That next day Malachi called me early in the morning.

"Morning Dunc," I said. "Is something wrong with you calling this early."

"You better believe there's something wrong," Malachi replied.

"What is it?" I asked concerned with the serious tone in his response.

"Why in the world were you up at Bee Cave last night?"

"Bee Cave? What are you talking about? I wasn't up there last night. You know what goes on up there. I'm a married man and my wife is in Gaffney."

"That's my concern."

"All right, quit joking around. What's really going on?"

"I got a call early this morning from somebody who didn't tell me who they were. I believe it was one of the local police. They just told me they saw your car up there last night, and it isn't the kind of place a minister who just got married should be hanging out."

"Did you tell them that you knew it probably wasn't me."

"Yeah, but they took the license plate number and it was your car."

Suddenly it hit me. "Grady had my car last night," I said. "You know he thinks he's the lady's man. I wouldn't put it past him to go up there."

"Well, unless he has some way to let the locals know that he has your car, you'd better tell him to stay away from that location with your car. You know these folks would love to catch you cheating on your wife. It would fit some of their images of what a preacher does."

"Soon as he gets up," I scowled, now angry because Grady apparently was messing around in my car. We did have that talk in not so pleasant a tone from both of us. But he understood whenever he drove my car that kind of behavior was not acceptable. I never had that problem again.

That summer had been the most fulfilling of my life. But when Latta told me that he was going to accept a place in the fall 1952 divinity class at Colgate University in New York, I felt as I had when he told me he wouldn't be attending Benedict when we first graduated from Sims. He was going to pursue an academic career in the ministry. Malachi and I decided to concentrate on the practical aspects of the ministry, while our friend decided to pursue the theoretical through graduate school. It didn't matter because we would always be close friends; three men who grew up in the small rural town of Union, and now were college graduates and on their way to fulfilling careers.

As college graduates we recognized that we represented only a small segment of the Black ministry. Most were only high school graduates if they even had reached that level. Our responsibility was now to prepare for the real world and all its problems that our people confronted in a racist society. We knew change was coming and had to prepare to play a major role in that change. That was the challenge we accepted, and many times in the years to come our commitment was tested.

By the end of the summer most of the members who had stayed away from Bethel for a few months, eventually returned where they belonged. But while they were absent, I conducted an aggressive and successful recruiting effort for new members. In fact, Bethel was the fastest growing Black church in the city and in Northern South Carolina. We were a young, progressive church that naturally attracted what many referred to as the New Negroes. That is people who had jettisoned the old way of thinking and felt there was nothing our race could not accomplish. We were determined not to be hindered by racism and the apartheid system. We were equipped to walk right around it, and leave those racist to fester in their own ignorance. But when confronted, we would use our collective effort as a church to fight back. Because my congregation strongly believed that their leader should be out front in our fight for equality, they were pleased to know the person they chose to lead them fit that role perfectly.

I stayed at the Lukesville School for two years and finally got the opportunity to teach at home in Union. The principal at Macbeth Elementary School was my fourth grade teacher when I was a young boy there. He was thrilled to hire one of their own to teach fifth grade classes. After I left Lukesville, I often wondered what happened to Billy. Did he get a chance to go to high school and college, or did he end up like many of those children as sharecroppers or doing menial jobs around the mill like their parents?

Finally, after two years at Macbeth, Sims High hired me as the school's vice-principal and classroom instructor. I taught French and mathematics to all grades. During the years I was in the classroom and vice-principal there, I never lost my vision and that was to build Bethel to the biggest and most respected church in Gaffney.

17.

After the first year, Rubye and I moved into the parsonage right next to the church. Finally, we were able to set up our household as husband and wife. It felt real good to be living with my wife in our first home. I was twenty-four years old, a college graduate and pastor of a rapidly growing church. My life was now settling into an acceptable pattern for me.

Since I now lived in Gaffney my schedule changed. I had to drive to Union everyday and then back home. I really didn't mind because it gave me more time at the church, and after all that was my priority. I was up every morning at five and out of the house by six so that I could be at the school by eight. Ruby was also teaching at Granard High School in Gaffney, so she was also up early in the morning.

There had always been a serious rivalry between Sims and Granard. Rubye coached the girl's basketball team at her school and whenever they traveled to Sims to play each other, she treated me like I was a stranger. When I walked into the gym, she totally ignored me. I would go over to their bench and say hello but would get a stern stare in return. Rubye was no nonsense, and she set aside the fact that we were married during those hours when her girls were in stiff competition with the girls from Sims.

We were adjusting quite well to each other, and had set our sights on starting a family. She knew that would interrupt her career as a teacher, but she was a strong Black woman and could be both a teacher and a mother. I loved her for that strength and the beauty she possessed in the image of generations of Black mothers.

Finally, it happened. That October, my life changed forever when I received her call. I was going to be a father.

"I believe it's time," Rubye calmly said to me on the phone. I was at the church preparing my sermon for that Sunday when the call came through on a hot April day in 1953.

"What?" I not so calmly replied. "Are you sure?"

"Yes, I'm sure, now you need to get over here and get me to the hospital," she scowled this time. "It's not the most pleasant feeling to have a baby."

"I'm on my way," I shouted. "Hold on, I'm on my way." I ran out of the church office, jumped into my car and headed home to pick up Rubye and take her to the hospital. I was about to become a father and I wasn't handling the situation quite as well as my wife. She was the calm one and I was the nervous wreck.

I sped into the parking lot at Cherokee Memorial Hospital in Gaffney. I parked the car, ran to the passenger side and helped Rubye out. I practically carried her up the steps and into the hospital. As we made our way down the corridor, I shouted.

"I need a nurse, I need a nurse."

A nurse who happened to be passing by rushed up to me.

"Is she all right?" she asked.

"No, she's getting ready to have a baby."

All this time, Rubye was quiet as she bent over and held her stomach.

"She's all right." The nurse smiled at me. "It must be your first child?"

"Yes it is," I said.

"Well you just go through the doors over there," she pointed to double doors down the hall. "That's where all fathers wait. There's coffee, juice, and water. You can sit down and relax." She took Rubye by the arm and led her straight ahead down the hall. "She'll be all right. Before you know it, you'll be a father."

I swung the door to the waiting room opened, found a seat not occupied by any of the four other men inside and sat down.

The Life of Reverend James W. Sanders

This was the beginning of a new chapter in my life. At twenty-five years old I was about to be a father. I prayed silently that God would give me the strength and guidance to be a good one. I closed my eyes and relaxed. A couple hours later the nurse swung the door open and said.

"Reverend Sanders come and see your baby daughter."

I followed her out the door and down the hall. A broad smile covered my face. I had a daughter and most important, Rubye and I had shared the most important part of any marriage. We had a child between us, and she would be an extension of who we are for a very long time, even after we are gone. I walked into the room, confident that we had produced a new life on earth who would forever be a child of God.

As I stared down at the innocence of my first born while she slept in her crib, I recognized that she was born free of the evil that existed in the world all around her at that time. I swore to God that Jewette, as well as any other children we brought into this world, would never experience the evil taint of racism in their lives. And the battles that I fought for my children against the system would also benefit the entire race.

The first of those battles began the next year in May 1954, when the United States Supreme Court ruled in the Brown V. Board of Education case that "separate was not equal." I knew the court would soon make a ruling since they had agreed to hear the case back in 1952. We were all proud in South Carolina because the impetus for the challenge to segregated schools started back in 1949 when Harry Briggs from Sumter first filed suit in federal court.

I believe every Negro living in the south gathered around their televisions on May 17 waiting for the court decision. Rubye and I had just finished dinner. We settled down in front of the television while Jewette, now one year old, tottered between the two of us diverting our attention from the historical decision about to be made. As I watched my daughter in her bright red dress, with her matching hair bows, I knew today would effect her and any future children we might have. Jewette climbed up in my lap and kissed me on the cheek. At that moment I wondered exactly what would this historic decision mean for my baby girl? And also what it would mean for Rubye and me as educators. South Carolina was rapidly becoming known nationwide for its inferior educational system.

The state had actually had a robust educational system during Reconstruction and the University of South Carolina had actually admitted its first black student in 1873, but in 1877 when southern whites took the government back, they shut the doors to Negroes. Today, with the court decision, our problems could either become better or worse. The commentator finally announced that in a unanimous decision the court ruled separate was not equal and that segregated schools were unconstitutional. The nine justices had overruled Plessy versus Ferguson which for fifty eight years had dictated that separate facilities was constitutional.

The Court also issued an implementation ruling that all the states must come up with a plan to integrate and added with "all deliberate speed." But the court ruling went on to state, "Full implementation of these constitutional principles may require solutions of varied local school problems. School authorities have the primary responsibility for elucidating, assessing, and solving these problems." The Court essentially gave the very groups that were opposed to desegregation the authority and responsibility to come up with plans to carry out the order. That was like asking the fox to guard the hen house.

Right after the court decision to desegregate the schools, our Senior Senator Strom Thurmond, signed a Southern Manifesto circulating among southern elected officials. The Manifesto pledged that the states of the South would use every available tool at their disposal to prevent the integration of the schools. It was at that point in my life that I knew the time had come for me to enter the battle for social change. I would have to call on all the skills and ability taught me by Prof. Sims, Reverend Zimmerman, Reverend A. C. Duncan and especially my Granddad and Poppa, to take on the battle that was about to begin.

Less than a week after the Court handed down its implementation ruling, one of the members of the school board visited me in my office at Sims High School. Over the years I had come to cautiously accept compliments from whites because usually behind the compliment was the dagger. That was the case when Ben Ryan sat across from me and began the conversation, with praise for my work.

"James," he started in his deep southern drawl. "We are so proud of you because the good work you're doing as Vice-Principal here at Sims High School. We're so pleased that a local, home-grown boy is heading up the education effort in our city."

"Thank you, sir," I said.

There was silence. I knew he was waiting for me to ask why he wanted to meet with me. I refused to give him the satisfaction. I would just wait him out. Finally, he broke the silence.

"I hear that you also pastor a church over in Gaffney. Is that true?"

"Yes it is," I answered. "Been their pastor going on two years now."

"Do you think that's a good thing for you to be doing while serving as Vice-Principal here at the school?"

"I don't see how one affects the other."

"We're not sure you can give the time and effort into being one of the leaders of the school if you have the responsibility to pastor a church?"

I could feel my blood rushing toward the top of my head. I tried to control my emotions. This white man had a lot of nerve trying to tell me the extent of my ability.

"Since church is primarily on Sunday and most other activities are in the evening, I don't see how there is a conflict."

"Some members of the board see differently?"

"Are you here to give me an ultimatum?" I asked.

"No, not yet. But you really should consider giving up your pastor's job."

"Being a pastor is my priority over all other things," I snapped. "That is my calling, and it is my commitment to God and I will never give up being pastor."

"Then let me suggest to you that you not use your position as a minister to delve into issues that aren't your concern. Things been fine here in the south for a very long time, and we ain't looking for them to change. Do you know what I'm saying to you?"

"I hear what you're saying," I answered.

"Then good we understand each other and there won't be any problems, right?"

"I guess not."

He got up and without saying another word turned and walked out of my office.

I knew exactly what his message was to me. The battle lines were being drawn, and the south was about to rally its allies and identify its enemies as they braced for a possible confrontation with the Supreme Court over its decision. They were lining up their friends and their enemies. Satisfied with my answer, he put me in the friend category for now. That would soon end, even if it meant I had to give up my teaching position. I was determined to preach a social gospel as Prof. Sims, Reverend Duncan and Reverend Zimmerman had taught me to do. There was no backing away from my responsibility to stand up for equality and justice in South Carolina.

The schools were not the only battlegrounds where the fight would occur. There were two movie theaters in Gaffney, the Capri and Hamrick. Blacks were not allowed in the Capri at all and could only sit in the balcony at the Hamrick. The Laundromat was also segregated, as were all the buses, restaurants, parks, and anywhere there was the potential for race mixing, including the church. And there was always the possibility of violence. What the white South did not recognize is that violence is never a deterrent to a race of people determined to be totally free. At some point, the violence no longer matters.

That was happening in the South and it all came to a head in August 1955, one month before my second child, James Jr., was born. Emmitt Till was lynched in Money, Mississippi for nothing more than talking fresh to a white woman. A fifteen-year old boy's life had been taken just like it had no meaning at all. But it had meaning to Mamie Till. That courageous lady made sure the entire country saw what evil did to her son. When she got his body back to Chicago, she had an open casket funeral, even though she had told the authorities in Mississippi that she would keep it closed. The two men that murdered Emmitt stood trial in Money, Mississippi but were found not guilty. As usual two more white men killed a Black and got away with it, because whites did not put any value on the life of a Black person.

I cringed when I stared at Emmitt's picture in *Jet* magazine. His face was distorted from the beating and the time he spent in the bottom of the river. The question that every Black man had to ask himself throughout the south is what would they do if that happened to their child. If someone harmed Jewette or James would I have the courage of my conviction not to lash out at the perpetrator? Non-violence was the foundation of the Christian religion, and those who preached the Gospel of Jesus Christ were compelled to live by its creed. I could only pray that I would never be put to that kind of test.

That brutal crime set off an entire movement just waiting for its catalyst. Just as Christ's death was the beginning of the greatest religious movement in history, Emmett Till's began the most significant social movement in America's young history.

Three months after the brutal murder in Mississippi, a brave Black woman refused to give up her seat on a bus in Montgomery, Alabama. When the bus driver demanded that Rosa Parks give a white rider her seat, she asked him and the authorities when they boarded the bus with intention to arrest her "why do you all continue to treat us this way?" She wasn't just talking about her, but nearly one hundred years after emancipation, the terrible treatment our people received in their country.

When I read her words in the paper, I immediately reflected back on Prof. Sims and his answer when we asked him why German prisoners could eat where we were not allowed. He told us that change would come, and it would be within our lifetime. We must not allow that kind of treatment to continue. My generation was the descendants of great men who had endured much abuse just to get us to this place. With the Montgomery Bus Boycott and the introduction of Dr. Martin Luther King Jr., a man of my generation, I knew it was time for us all to act. Ministers had to step out of the pulpit and into the streets for social action, in the name of the Lord.

One Thursday afternoon, I finished my day at Sims High

School and met Malachi at Reverend Zimmerman's office. We needed direction in just how much we should get involved in what was quickly becoming a movement throughout the South.

Reverend Zimmerman sat behind his big oak desk and began the conversation.

"Ministers must now look outside the walls of the church and into the streets," he began. "There is a social movement, based on the Gospel of Jesus Christ, now underway."

"The question is do you think our people are ready?" I asked. I leaned forward in my chair as if that would help me take in his answer.

"It's your job to get them ready," he said. "The clergy has always been the leaders in the Negro community simply because they had the independence that was needed in order to lead. God has chosen Martin to begin the movement, now it is time for all of us to join and support him." He paused to let us absorb what he was saying. "It is no coincidence that Vernon Johns preceded Martin as the minister at Dexter Avenue Baptist Church there in Montgomery. Vernon stepped out into the street long before anyone else, and was penalized for it. His people were not yet ready, and then God sent them Martin as a sign that it was time to get ready. And that is a sign that we all must yield to and begin the movement. This will be a crusade for justice, and who better to lead it than us. After all Jesus spoke of justice and demonstrated His commitment to it many times."

"Do you plan to get involved?" Malachi asked.

"It's your turn," Reverend Zimmerman said. "My job as it was A. C. Duncan's job was to bring you all up in such a way that you could expand the ministry further than where we took it. We were there when our people were beaten, raped, and sometimes lynched. We offered comfort to the families and helped sustain some semblance of order and respect for us. Now it is your turn to take this to another level. That is the purpose of each generation. You must carry out your mandate from God. This is your mandate, so you young men go out and do what God insists you must do."

On the drive back over to Gaffney, Reverend Zimmerman's words continued to resonate with me. Is this what God had in mind for me when He sent me the message back at Sims High School when I was only fifteen? Not only was I to preach his word, but also demonstrate my commitment to it through social action. I rushed into the house and Rubye stared at me as if to ask what happened to you.

"Get our dirty clothes together, put them in a laundry bag," I said.

"Do what?"

"Put them in a laundry bag for me," I repeated.

"What are you going to do?" Rubye asked.

"I'm going to integrate the Laundromat over on Tenth Street."

"Rev, what you trying to prove?" she asked

"That as a minister of God, I am not going to restrict my actions to inside the church on Sundays only. I am going to stand up for what is right, and that isn't what's happening here in Gaffney or anywhere in the south."

"You know these white folks go crazy when Negroes challenge their way of living. The Ku Klux Klan marched just last week outside Gaffney. What you trying to do, get yourself killed?"

"No Rubye I'm not trying to get myself killed, but I am going to get myself right with the Lord. We have to make a stand and we have to do it now. No more waiting for tomorrow. It has to be done now, so please get those clothes for me and I'll be back right after I finish washing them."

Rubye packed some diapers into a white laundry bag and handed it to me.

"Makes no sense to me, but do what you think is right," she said.

"I'll be all right," I said. "God wants me to do this, and if God wants me to do it, who can stand against me." I kissed her and headed out the door.

I drove straight to the Laundromat. During the drive I thought of Dr. King leading the boycott in Montgomery, and how he had introduced a new strategy of non-violence as the most effective way to fight violence. I pulled into the parking lot on the side of the Laundromat, grabbed my clothes bag and headed toward my first major confrontation with segregation.

"Wait just a minute," the white attendant shouted as I strolled inside and began to load my clothes into a washing machine. "What you thing you doing?"

"Obviously washing my clothes," I replied.

"You know y'all ain't allowed in here. "

I anticipated the rejection but had to go through with the attempt. I loaded my clothes into the bag, turned and started back out of the building.

"I will be back," I scowled. "And next time with more people and more people and more people until you finally realize that God means for this place to serve all His children."

With that initial rejection, my commitment to the defeat of an apartheid system in Gaffney and throughout South Carolina had begun. I was determined it would not end until all vestiges of that evil and wicked system were eradicated from our city, our state, and our country.

18.

It had been over two years since I'd seen Latta, so when he called and told me he was home for the Christmas break in 1956 I arranged to meet him in Union on the Saturday a week before Christmas. We met at Corinth; that seemed to be the place for reunions. Reverend Zimmerman gave us his office for a couple hours. He had to make hospital visits. When we met at the church, we hugged just as any two long lost friends would do. Once settled in, Latta told me a story about his initial introduction to going to Colgate.

The Divinity School at Colgate made it a requirement that advanced graduate students act as mentor to a new student entering the program at the graduate level. A senior year graduate student from North Carolina sent out an announcement throughout North and South Carolina asking if there was a student from either state who might be entering the graduate program. He indicated that he would be willing to serve as their mentor, and they would be welcomed to drive back to New York with him when it was time to go.

Latta read the announcement and responded. They corresponded for the rest of the summer, and then when it was time to head for school, the young man instructed Latta to take the Greyhound Bus to Clinton, North Carolina, a small rural town close to his parent's farm. He provided Latta with a telephone number he should call once he got to the town. The number was that of a friend, who would then go to the mentor's house and let him know that Latta was at the Greyhound station. At the stop just before Clinton, Latta called the man and let him know he would be there within the next two hours.

When the bus arrived in Clinton, the driver swung the door open and some of the passengers got off. Latta, sitting in the back of the bus had to wait for all the white people to get off first, then he got up and started toward the front. Before he got all the way up to the front door, a young white man boarded the bus, looked all around and then turned and left.

Latta then got off the bus and took a seat for Coloreds. He waited over an hour and then decided to call the number again. After talking with the man, informing him that he was there and still waiting for someone to pick him up, he sat back down. About an hour later a car drove up, and the same white man who had boarded the bus earlier, parked and got out of the car. He looked over at the telephone booth, and looked at Latta.

"Did you see another man around here about an hour ago?" he asked.

"No, I've been here for over two hours and everybody that got off the bus is now gone."

A serious look spread across the man's face. He reluctantly said. "I'm looking for someone named Latta Thomas."

"That's me," Latta said.

Now the look was very somber. "Are you serious?"

"Just as serious as I can be."

Slowly the man extended his hand toward me. "Well, I'm Boone," he said as I took his hand and we shook. "Most of my friends call me Daniel Boone, you know like the great American outdoors man. You can just call me Boone."

We released our grip and there was a moment of silence. I don't believe he knew exactly what he wanted to say.

"I guess I just took for granted you were white," he finally said. "Let's get going. You're going to spend the night at my parent's home out in the country." He paused for a moment as we both climbed inside the car. "Tonight for the first time in their lives, my parents will experience my way of thinking. This is going to be very interesting."

I had to interrupt his story because of the bizarre nature of it. I asked Latta, "Didn't you know that you were corresponding with someone white?"

A broad smile spread across his face and there was a rather mischievous twinkle in his eyes.

"I figured he was probably white simply because I didn't know of any other Negroes from the south at Colgate. I would be the first one in years, so yes, I knew he was white."

"Since he didn't know you were a Negro, I guess his parents didn't either. And he told you that you'd be spending the night at his home," I said. "Where were you going to sleep, in the dog house? Or maybe they still had some slave quarters on the property?" We both laughed.

"No, not all," Latta said. "Let me get back to the story. It gets better."

"Yes, do that cause I have to hear this."

"When we got to the home, his parents had already gone to bed. He took me to the spare bedroom that was downstairs close to the living room and the front door. He told me that was the first time a Negro had been in the front part of their home, let alone in one of the bedrooms, and definitely would be the first time that one spent the night in their home. I wasn't afraid at all nor was I nervous. In fact it gave me somewhat of a rush not knowing exactly how his parents would respond in the morning when they knew a Negro had spent the night inside their home. I went to bed and slept quite well.

The next morning when I got up and dressed, I looked out the window and saw his father at the barn feeding the animals. Feeling rather bold, I decided to go out there and introduce myself to him, not knowing if Boone had told him about me yet. As I approached the old man, I knew this could go either way. I needed to establish some commonality between us. I noticed how tall and good his corn was and that would be my talking point.

"Good morning Mr. Boone," I said but did not extend my hand for him to shake. That would have been too bold. "My name is Latta Thomas and I'll be entering Colgate Divinity School. Your son has agreed to be my mentor."

He didn't stop feeding the animals. He didn't even look at me, just kept feeding the stock.

"Mr. Boone I grew up on a farm right outside Union, South Carolina and I got to say that is some mighty good corn you got there, sir. Better than what I ever saw."

Mr. Boone finally looked at me. A slight smile crossed his face. I had paid him a complement and that made all the difference in the world. White folks expected Negroes to complement them and show them respect.

"So you're a good old country boy," Mr. Boone said.

"Yes sir, I sure am," I said.

"Now you going to be a preacher?"

"Yes sir, I sure am."

"Good, your people need more good preachers."

"I know sir, and I look forward to serving the Lord."

"It's a noble profession, that is serving the Lord."

"Yes sir, I plan to go right back to Union, South Carolina when I graduate and spread the word of God to my people. I already have two very close friends who are ministers in that area. We all graduated from Benedict College in Columbia, South Carolina, and they both have churches."

"Best of luck to you," Mr. Boone said. He threw the last handful of feed to the animals, then turned and walked back toward the house. I followed close behind him.

Mrs. Boone turned out to be much friendlier than her husband. She had prepared breakfast for us but told me that I could not eat at the table with them. Instead, they set up a place for me right outside the kitchen. They were only willing to break southern tradition to a certain extent.

After breakfast, Daniel and I packed our belongings and headed out for New York. When we left, Daniel's parents congratulated me on getting into graduate school and wished me the best of luck. We drove off and I probably won't ever see them again in life. But what happened that night is something that all of us will remember for a very long time. In a very quiet and private way we had broken the rules of segregation and no one was hurt. We all were the better off for the experience."

"How'd it make you feel having to eat in a separate room from the rest of them?" I asked.

"I really didn't think much about it. The fact that I'd actually slept inside their home without the Ku Klux Klan showing up, far outweighed where I had to eat. And anyway, the food was delicious and that also was more important than where I had to eat."

"What happened when you got to Colgate?" I asked.

"When the other students heard about my experience I was somewhat a hero for the first few weeks. To them that was a major breakthrough in terms of race relations and proof that we could overcome the stupid customs of the south."

"Are you close to Daniel now?"

"Yes, as a matter of fact just before I left to come home for Christmas break, he told me that his parents confided in him that my staying in their home had changed their attitude about Negroes, somewhat."

"I assume for the better?" I asked.

"Absolutely. I believe that there is room for change," Latta said. His expression changed. He was serious. "Daniel is about our age and was raised in the south but his attitude about race relations is different," he continued. "He kept saying that now his parents would have to see things his way when he picked me up. And he didn't back down. His attitude helped change his parents' feelings about race."

"Are you saying that as a result of your visiting them, they have changed?" I asked with some doubt.

"No, not at all," he shot back at me. "But it did make them think about the issue and that's a good start."

"I guess you got a point," I said as we got up and prepared to leave. "We have some very exciting times in front of us, and I just pray that we all will be prepared for what is coming in the future."

"From what I see happening among young whites we won't be

alone. They know change must come, and they will probably be right on the front line with us when it happens.

"I pray that's true because we sure will need them. I have to get back over to Gaffney. The children are preparing for their Christmas program. If you get a chance you should come on over to the church for Christmas service."

"I'll try my best."

We shook hands and I started back over to Gaffney. Latta never did make it over to the Christmas service. In fact, I didn't get a chance to see him before he left going back to school. It would be years before I saw him again. When he graduated from Colgate he remained up North as pastor of a number of churches in New York. But as the civil rights issue heated up in Gaffney I often thought about him and his experience with his friend Boone and his parents.

In the fall of 1957, our third child, Ruzlin was born. She also was a healthy baby but unlike Jewette and James, she had very powerful vocal chords and didn't mind letting us hear them when she was hungry. We now had three children and I began to feel an urgent need for change. I didn't want my children to grow up in the same kind of racist environment that Rubye and I did. It would be wonderful if we could just pray all prejudice away and the world would be as close to perfect as it possibly could be here on earth. But that was not the case and it again was made quite apparent when nine Black students attempted to integrate Central High School in Little Rock, Arkansas.

It had been three years since the Brown V. Board of Education Supreme Court decision overturning separate but equal doctrine and still no schools in the south were integrated. The test case took place in Little Rock, Arkansas in the fall of 1957. Through the brave work of the NAACP and a bold woman, Daisy Bates, nine Black students had enrolled at the all white Central High School. The first day they showed up for classes, the white people were so crazy with hatred that they had to turn back. A week later, President Dwight Eisenhower sent the Air National Guard to the school to help accompany the Black students to their classes. It worked and they actually did attend class. Eventually most of them dropped out, but Ernest Green did manage to graduate that spring, making him the first Black student to graduate from an all white high school after the Brown decision. However, like the rest of the south there had been no movement at all to integrate the schools in Gaffney. It would be years before Gaffney would comply with the court decision.

< The Spiritual Journey of a Legend >

19.

It surprised no one that Gaffney, as well as the entire state of South Carolina, had not integrated the schools or any other venues where segregation existed. The most blatant blemish on the south was the denial of the right to vote for over five million Blacks, and South Carolina was one of the worst states of all. As the election of 1960 loomed on the horizon we considered which of the two candidates, Richard Nixon the Republican or John Kennedy the Democrat, would support the right for us to vote. Nixon hoped to win some support from the south because Kennedy was a Catholic and no Catholic candidate had ever won high office in the south. Kennedy did not want to alienate the very delicate balance that made up the Democratic coalition and depended on the south for support. To advocate for the vote for Blacks in the south, could possibly send the whites over to the Republican Party. Kennedy made two strategic moves to assure that the white south voted for him, while still maintaining a hold on the Black vote up north that had slowly been moving to the Democratic Party, as a result of President Franklin Roosevelt's New Deal policies.

In order to hold on to the white south, he chose a southerner, Senator Lyndon Baines Johnson, as his vice-presidential running mate. That assured him of the vote from Texas and other parts of the south. The other strategic move he made affected every minister in the south, and led to a flooding of northern Black votes to the Democratic Party.

In summer 1960, Dr. Martin Luther King, Jr. was arrested in Georgia and detained in the Dekalb County Jail. In the middle of the night he was shackled and taken to Reidsville Maximum

Security Prison. Shocked that her husband was in a maximum-security prison from a charge of an outstanding ticket, Coretta Scott-King solicited the support from the Republican Presidential Candidate, Richard Nixon who refused to return her call. But surprisingly, she did receive a call from Senator John Kennedy who promised to do whatever was possible to get her husband out of the prison. One day later, Robert Kennedy questioned how the judge could deny King bail on a misdemeanor, and why he was locked in a maximum-security prison. We were following these developments closely, and when our ministerial alliance found out that Kennedy had intervened on behalf of King we immediately threw all our support behind him.

With Kennedy's election we held out hope that change would soon come throughout the south. However, our hopes were somewhat dashed by the rash of violence that engulfed the country during the bloody and turbulent year of 1963.

By spring 1963, the struggle to break down apartheid throughout the South increased considerably. The impetus had come three years earlier in 1960, when a number of young Black students from North Carolina A and T, Rubye's alma mater, decided they would sit at the counter at the Five and Dime Store in Raleigh. These students were an extension of us when we wanted to take a stand back in 1949 at Benedict. I supported their effort, and even sent a little money to help them keep up their fight. I especially admired young John Lewis, a youthful preacher, who became the leader of their group as they expanded from North Carolina into Georgia and other Southern states. This was the generation of young people right behind my generation, and they now had carried the struggle to a new dimension. Whereas we talked about doing something, they actually did. And this was the way that Prof. Sims said it would happen. Every new generation would expand the movement slowly until eventually all barriers of an anachronistic system would be eradicated.

During the summer of 1963, it became considerably clear that the anachronistic system would not go away quietly. The segregationists would use any means necessary to maintain their dominance over us. Since Reconstruction, the white majority had no problems using violence as a means to intimidate Black people throughout the south. In June of that year the first of three brutal acts occurred.

The Life of Reverend James W. Sanders

It was Tuesday evening that I received a telephone call from Malachi. I could detect the frustration, mixed with a little bit of anger in his voice.

"I just got word that some white racist assassinated the head of the NAACP in Jackson, Mississippi," he said.

I cringed for a moment, closed my eyes and said a short prayer.

"You there Sanders?" he asked.

"Yeah, I'm here," I said. "Who was he?" I asked.

"A man named Medgar Evers. He was president of the Jackson branch of the NAACP. They shot him right in his driveway as he got out of his car."

"Oh, my God," I scowled. "Did his family see it?"

"No, but they rushed out to the driveway when they heard the shots. Myrlie, his wife, cradled his body in her arms as though she could pass life from her back into him. What is wrong with these people, Sanders, what's wrong with them?"

"Decades of hate," I said more subdued. "Let us pray for Brother Medgar and his family." We prayed and then hung up the phone.

The more determined Negroes were to eradicate segregation the more desperate white bigots became, and their resolve to use violence if necessary also increased. First they killed Medgar in Mississippi and then they turned their violence against children in Birmingham.

Rubye and I sat in the living room and watched on television as the police brutality unfolded in what was considered the most segregated city in the south. It was mid-morning as the marchers walked out of the Sixteenth Street Baptist Church and across the street into the park where they assembled for their protest. On one of the other corners, the police lined up with helmets covering their face and their nightclubs at the ready position. Eugene Bull Connors, the Birmingham Police Commissioner, stood next to his white colored tank he often used to patrol the Black community, and shouted to the crowd.

"I'm giving you five minutes to disperse, then I'm loosening

171

the dogs and turning on the water hose."

The crowd consisted mostly of women and children. They were the only ones that could afford to demonstrate since the men had to work and possibly get fired for participating in what Governor George Wallace had designated as disobeying the laws of the state of Alabama.

Connors finally did give the order to attack and all bedlam broke loose. Women and children were trying to escape the vicious bites from the dogs, and the torrent strength of the water from the hoses. People began screaming and crying. I watched on in horror.

But I also watched on with more determination than before to continue fighting to integrate all facets of life in Gaffney. Our ministerial alliance agreed that if King and the other ministers could withstand the threat of violence and continue to fight, we must do the same. As ministers we put our safety in God's hands and if He was with us no man could harm us.

While we continued to struggle with the problem of integration during the summer of 1963, Dr. Martin Luther King, Jr. planned a march on Washington D. C. to emphasize the importance of integrating, not only the schools in the south, but all other segregated institutions. It was also billed as a march for jobs and better living conditions for the poor. He was sending his emissaries out to meet with different ministerial groups to discuss participating.

Malachi and I discussed going, but our schedules wouldn't allow us to leave. In fact, I was so engrossed in the battle to integrate Gaffney Schools that my mind was totally pre-occupied with that problem the day of King's speech at the Lincoln Monument.

Rubye and I sat glued to the television as we watched the rally on the mall and listened intently to Dr. King's ending of his speech, which contained the "I have a dream" portion. Like most other people, I was moved by his stimulating words when he told the world that we all would be free someday. But what I enjoyed most of all, was the earlier part of the speech when he spoke of the un-cashed check. All Negroes were in possession of an un-cashed check of promises from this government and country. He told millions of people listening that someday the country would have to pay up and provide Negroes with all the rights as every other American citizen.

The Life of Reverend James W. Sanders

As I listened to him speak, my mind was carried back to that time when Prof. Sims told us in class that we would be the generation to make a difference, and that a special leader was on the way to help us make it through. I recognized, at that moment, I was looking and listening to that leader. Dr. King's words gave me the energy to continue fighting on. But if they weren't enough to keep me energized, what happened the next month was.

It was a hot September Sunday and Bethel was packed. Every week we were filling the pews as congregations throughout the South were experiencing extremely high attendance because of what was happening in places like Birmingham and other hot civil rights spots. Fortunately, Gaffney had been free from any kind of disturbance. Still, we felt that battles in other parts of the region were our battles also. I sat back down from leading an altar call and the choir was singing when one of the deacons strolled up to me and whispered.

"Reverend, there has been an awful explosion in Birmingham, Alabama at the Sixteenth Street Baptist Church."

I turned and stared at him. They were an hour behind us in time so that meant the explosion must have gone off during Sunday school.

"Was there anyone in the church?" I asked but really knew the answer.

"Yes," he again whispered. "It was filled with children having Sunday school."

My immediate thoughts were for the parents, who must be in a panic rushing to the church trying to find their children. I quickly glanced out at my three children sitting in the first row with Rubye. I couldn't even start to imagine the turmoil running through the families in Birmingham.

"Let me know if you get any additional information before church is out," I said and the deacon turned and went out the side door to get an update.

The deacon never came back with an update. The service went as usual. I decided not to mention it to the congregation without a complete report on the damage, and if there were any fatalities. Once the service was over, we were made aware of the serious damage done that day. Four little girls had been brutally murdered by some evil feigns. We also found out that later in the day, two young boys were killed as a follow up to the damage done at the church.

That evening I called Reverend C. V. Owens, who was an old friend and also a minister in Gaffney. We knew that King would be preaching the service for the young girls.

"How is he going to convince those people that they have to stay on course, and that non-violence is the only way for us as a people?" I asked.

"I got word today that some of the folks already organizing vigilante groups to hunt down the murderers," C.V. said.

"Negroes all over this country and especially up North going to be calling for all of us to arm ourselves and start fighting back. Some already done moved over to the Nation of Islam as an alternative to what we do as Christian ministers," I said.

"No way we can lose focus and support any other method than the one set out by Dr. King. I plan to reiterate that very fact on Sunday morning," C.V. added.

"We have to do more than what we been doing." I squeezed the phone tightly in the grip of my right hand. "The Association has to take stronger stands and we must stick together and begin to force change here in Gaffney."

"You know I'm with you James as are all the ministers. You are our Dr. King here in this part of South Carolina, and we'll back you all the way."

C. V.'s encouraging words were refreshing. They provided me with the strength to increase the pressure on Gaffney to break down all barriers of segregation within the city. I refused to allow the city to practice a South African form or apartheid in a state that I loved and felt an intricate part of my entire life.

It was at this time that I met Jack Millwood when a young man who belonged to my church had been accidently killed working on Jack's father's farm. The entire Millwood family attended the funeral and we invited them to sit with the young man's family right in the front row. Jack and I were the two staunchest supporters for change. He was one of the few white Southerners who recognized that conditions had to change throughout the South for the good of the country. He acknowledged that both slavery and apartheid were an evil and that unless the South changed its ways, then a greater punishment would be inflicted on it. After the funeral we began to talk about how we could prevent that from happening in our own small way.

Jack was selected to head up a biracial council looking into ways that we could integrate the Gaffney Public Schools without racial disturbance. He asked me to serve on that council. I agreed, and that began a friendship that would survive some very intense battles with those forces determined not to change the way of life they felt was a tradition, and best for all races. We argued with the other members of the Biracial commission that we must act fast to comply with Brown Supreme Court decision.

Our biggest opposition was from the Cherokee County Board of Education. They had strong support from the elected officials, who had pledged to fight integration with every legal tool available to them. Strom Thurmond, who had changed parties and was now a Republican, was the leading senator opposed to integration and he was from our state. With that kind of support behind them, the Board of Education believed they could wait this out and it would soon pass.

All the southern states were doing whatever they could to prevent implementation of the court order. The state of Virginia threatened to close down the entire school system. Battles between those who wanted to come to some kind of amiable agreement and the others adamantly opposed had already occurred in that state. Two years later, the governor closed down their public schools in that state. No doubt, the majority of the white South was united in opposition to integration.

Now with three children, the urgency of living in the racist south began to work on me. The very worst aspect of segregation was when a parent had to explain to a child why they couldn't drink from a fountain, eat at a lunch counter, go into a movie theater or had to ride on the back of the bus. As Jewette, James, and Ruzlin became conscious of the fact that we were considered different and treated differently than whites, I knew that was a topic I must discuss with them.

I felt that way as I pulled into the driveway after a heated debate with the Gaffney School Board. I knew it was time to have a discussion with the children. Just like my father had done with Nette, Grady and me, we assembled in the living room and I explained to them the unfortunate evil they would confront as they grew up in the south.

I told them they were as good as any one else and that the whole system of segregation was unfair, but more important implemented by insecure people who used their power to abuse other people. No descendant of the Sanders' lineage should ever feel inferior. Their grandfather had confronted the evil when he helped a Black man and white woman in love escape to the north and their great grandfather had walked right into the middle of a mob set on lynching his brother. Because he stood tall and didn't back down, he saved his brother's life. I assured my three children that they were descendants of men and women with strong moral convictions, who respected the rights of others but refused to let others abuse them. Their success was based on a strong commitment to God and they always remained anchored in their religious beliefs.

I also made it a point to challenge the Capri Theater. I believed that my children should have the same opportunity to watch a movie anywhere they wanted as other children were allowed to do. They were children and it didn't bother them that they could not go to the Capri. They just wanted to see the movie. I knew, however, that psychologically it would eventually impact the way they thought of themselves. I finally decided to confront that demeaning practice. It was on a Saturday afternoon that I surprised them.

"You kids get ready," I said.

They had been in their bedrooms cleaning them up and were probably shocked that I told them to stop cleaning and get ready to go with me. I never interrupted their Saturday chores.

Rubye was also surprised. I hadn't told her what I planned to do.

"Rev, where you taking those kids?" she asked. "And why you stopping them from doing their chores?"

"To the movies," I blurted out.

Rubye walked into the living room where I was standing by the door waiting for the children.

"What'd you say?" she asked.

"To the movies," I repeated.

"You never let them go to the Hambrick. Do you feel all right?"

"Yes I feel fine, and we're not going to the Hambrick," I said.

"What you getting ready to do with my kids?"

"Prepare them for what is going to be in front of them in this crazy place."

"Rev, don't you get my kids hurt."

"They're not going to get hurt, but they are going to get a lesson in challenging evil and not accepting it."

Jewette, James and Ruzlin came out of their bedrooms and joined me at the front door.

"We're ready," Jewette said.

"Don't worry Rubye, it'll be all right," I said and the four of us headed out the door and into the car.

Ruzlin and Jewette got in the back seat of the car and James, Jr., sat up front. I drove across town and found a parking space across from the theater. Jewette and Ruzlin piled out of the backseat, James, Jr., the front seat and we all strolled across the street, and stood in front of the theater.

I approached the ticket master sitting in an enclosed small booth. Jewette, James, Jr. and Ruzlin were standing close to me anxiously waiting for something to happen.

"I'd like three children's tickets," I said.

"You know damn well you can't go in this theater," the man scowled. "Your people can only go to the Hambrick and even there you got to sit up in the balcony."

"My children will go to any theater in this city they wish to attend," I said.

"Daddy, we can't go in there," Jewette spoke up. I knew she

was nervous and probably a little bit frightened. But this was a lesson all three of them had to learn; you cannot back down to evil because if you do, it'll continue to control you.

"Quiet, Jewette," I shot back at her. "It'll be all right." I didn't mean to scold her but this was confrontation time.

"You cannot continue this silly nonsense. I will not allow you to embarrass and demean my children," I said.

"I don't make the rules," he now raised his voice. "If you don't want to take your children over to the Hambrick where they belong, then you can just leave cause you sure ain't going inside here."

"My children will soon sit in this theater. The time is coming so you best get ready," I said, and with the kids turned and walked away.

In October 1963 President Kennedy finally decided to act. It was a month after the tragic bombing at the Sixteenth Street Baptist Church in Birmingham, and the beginning of a new school year in which no integration had taken place. The president was now willing to put his presidency on the line for what he finally recognized had to be done at the national level.

Rubye and I gathered around the television as President Kennedy addressed the nation on the most important issue of the day..

He began, "We are confronted with a moral issue, It is as old as the Scriptures and as clear as the American Constitution. The heart of the question is whether all Americans are to be afforded equal rights and equal opportunities, whether we are going to treat our fellow Americans as we want to be treated."

His reference to Scripture brought a smile to my rather subdued feelings about what he would say and do. I knew he was reaching out to the better nature of the American people and that was the belief in a living and fair God.

He continued, "Now the time has come for this nation to fulfill its promise. The events in Birmingham and elsewhere have so increased the cries for equality that no city or state or legislative body can prudently choose to ignore them. We face, therefore, a moral crisis as a country and a people. A great change is at hand, and our task, our obligation is to make that revolution, that change, peaceful and constructive for all."

The President then told the entire nation that he would introduce civil rights legislation immediately to eradicate all semblance of inequality in the country. At that point I knew what Prof. Sims had told us years ago was about to happen and that the deliverer was staring me right in the face in the person of President Kennedy.

20.

"Mr. Sanders, the president has been shot in Dallas, Texas and they don't know if he's going to live," one of the younger teachers ran into my office at Sims High and shouted.

I stopped what I was doing and looked up at the teacher. "What?" was all I said.

"Yes, he's been rushed to a hospital. The governor of Texas was also wounded but not as bad as the president."

"How about the first lady?"

"She's fine, but the poor lady had to cradle the president's head in her lap all the way to the hospital. They say blood was all over her."

I swung my chair around and turned on the small radio I had on the credenza behind my desk. The teacher stood waiting to hear the latest report. We tuned in just in time to hear Walter Cronkite of CBS News say, "President John Kennedy died at 12:20 Central Standard Time. Let's all pray."

I turned back around and stared at the teacher in disbelief. My first thought was that Lyndon Johnson a southerner from Texas would be the new president. What would happen to the civil rights legislation that Kennedy had introduced in congress in October? That was less than a month ago, and now it would probably be dead.

"What's going to happen now Reverend Sanders?" the young teacher asked.

"I don't know but I do know that we must do as Walter Cronkite suggested and that is pray for our country."

Without another word spoken, the young teacher turned and strolled out of my office, with head bowed in sadness. I grabbed my phone and started to call Malachi, but then it dawned on me that he was probably in class. I thought to call C. V. but he was also in class, as was Rubye. So I clasped my hands together, bowed my head and prayed.

That Sunday, Bethel was packed for the morning service. Mourners of the president's death turned to the church for some kind of consolation. I knew that would be the case, so Saturday afternoon, as I prepared my sermon I concentrated on great leaders dying early before their work was complete. While the choir sang their introductory song before I rose to preach, I prayed that God would send the words that best fit the occasion as he had done in the past with the killing of the four little girls in Birmingham. That was only a couple months ago, and now we were addressing another unfortunate tragedy on a Sunday morning in Bethel. When I stood in front of my congregation I knew they looked to me for direction. As I began, I recognized that I was simply God's messenger.

"I know you all are wondering why we have to lose good leaders before their work is done here on earth. We lost President Abraham Lincoln before he finished his work on behalf of our ancestors. Now we have lost another great President in Kennedy and right at a time when he was about to make changes in the social structure, here in the South. But through God's grace and mercy, we will survive this tragedy. A leader we probably never expected to do God's bidding for us will do His work. I know that we don't feel too comfortable with a president from the south, the first one since before the civil war but we must always remember that Mr. Johnson is not in charge of this journey, God is and His will be done. We must always remember we serve a risen Savior, who is the only way to salvation and no one human being can change this world, without having Jesus Christ in their lives. Our battle is the same no matter what your race or what part of the country you come from. So let us pray for our new president that he will have the strength, knowledge, and love of God in his heart to do what is right for all God's children."

The Life of Reverend James W. Sanders

As we moved into the New Year, chances of implementing strategies to fight segregation seemed bleak. We knew that it could not be done without the national government's strong commitment to change. Our hope for change had been elevated when President Kennedy had announced his plans to have a civil rights bill introduced in Congress. Finally, our prayers for deliverance from decades, in fact, centuries of oppression were answered. We had two men in the image of Moses, and they were the two K's, King and Kennedy. But with the president's death, we lost one of our two men in the image of Moses, and feared that the man who would replace him in the White House would be like Pharaoh, a man who would undoubtedly push to turn back any progress that had been made up to that point. Johnson was the first president from the south since the civil war. He came from a state steeped heavily in racial bigotry and, despite his lukewarm support of the weak Civil Rights Act of 1957, he had an abysmal record on issues dealing with equality. Quite naturally, I was disappointed. But eventually my disappointment would turn to exhilarating joy as we moved into the summer of 1964.

The first indication that I might have misread the big Texan who talked with a drawl, happened when I attended a meeting in Atlanta, Georgia convened by the Southern Christian Leadership Conference. Joseph Lowery, one of King's key lieutenants, hosted the meeting. Over fifty ministers, most from Georgia, were there. I recognized a number of Baptists preachers from South Carolina, North Carolina and Florida in the room.

Lowery opened with a prayer and then got right to the reason we were all asked to attend the meeting.

"Martin has been in communication with the new president," he said. "And it looks like we may have misjudged this man."

"What are you talking about?" one of the ministers I didn't know blurted out. "He's from the south, and he opposed attempts to pass meaningful legislation all the time he was in the senate. He even opposed legislation to make lynching a federal crime."

"And he did that because Texas is one of the leading states when it comes to lynching," another minister added.

"Yes, but he had to do that in order to get elected in Texas," Lowery said.

"Now that he's president his constituency is the entire country," I said. "And if Kennedy believed that he could support civil rights and get re-elected, maybe Johnson now believes he can do the same."

"Yes, but Kennedy was doing it from a sincere belief that it was the right thing to do," the minister snapped. "He put principle before re-election."

"Hold on brothers," Lowery interjected. "You didn't let me get to my main point."

"Go ahead brother," another minister said.

"Thank you brothers. Martin has been briefed by the White House staff. They assured him that Johnson plans to push forward with the civil rights bill this summer."

"You mean he's going to do this during an election year?" I asked.

"Exactly," Lowery said. "He has told his staff that there will be a civil rights bill this summer, even if it means he'll lose the entire south and possibly the election. That is the same position President Kennedy had taken."

A minister who had been quiet all this time jumped to his feet. "He's only trying to outdo Kennedy. He wants to accomplish more than Kennedy did, just to prove to the world that he is a better president. You know the two men really didn't like each other. And word was spreading that the president was going to drop him from the ticket this year."

"Brothers," Lowery scowled. "I don't care why he's doing it, as long as it gets done."

"Joe's right," I said. "Our eyes have to stay on the prize and that is legislation that ends segregation for good in the south. And if the truth be told, we have a much better chance of getting that done with Johnson than we ever had with Kennedy."

"Why do you say that?" a minister I recognized but couldn't recall his name asked.

"Because Johnson was majority leader in the senate and knows better than anyone else where all the skeletons are buried.

If Johnson says he'll get it done, he will."

"That's right," Lowery said. "Word is spreading on Capitol Hill that if the southern senators try to filibuster then Johnson will leave the bill on the Senate floor until hell freezes over."

"He may be able to manipulate the senate," another minister from Florida joined in. "Because he knows dirt on all the senators, but what about the House of Representatives? "

"Democrats have an overwhelming majority in the House," Lowery replied. "He can afford to lose some Democratic votes but with enough Republican crossovers from up north and Democrats who will vote the straight party line, he can get it passed in the House."

"What I hear you all saying is that some good may have come out of the assassination of Kennedy last year," A minister from North Carolina said.

We were all silent for a moment. As ministers most of us probably had similar responses to that comment. I spoke up and provided a response that I felt would be satisfactory to Jesus.

"God will answer that question when we see the end results of the civil rights bill sometime this summer." I paused for a moment and then asked. "What is it Martin wants us to do?"

"First and most important, he wants us to pray," Lowery answered. "Then he wants us all to come together and support the president in his re-election bid. I know that most of our members can't vote, but they have relatives up north who can. Make sure they call them and make sure they are registered, and that they vote for the president. His opponent will be Senator Barry Goldwater from Arizona and he's already expressed his opposition to any civil rights legislation, based on a states rights argument."

"Is there any possibility that this bill will contain a voting rights provision?" another minister asked.

"No, not yet," Lowery said. "The president doesn't believe he can get both, that is eliminating segregation and a voting rights bill in the same year, and especially since this is an election year. He wants to break down the barriers to equality first."

"When will we get a voting rights bill?" the minister continued.

"Next," Lowery said. "Let's take one step at a time."

"I'm sure God is directing the president," I said. "And if the president says eliminating segregation is the first step then we should accept that."

"How do you know it's being directed by God?" a very young minister asked.

We all turned and glared at him with a message that a minister should never question God and His involvement in our affairs.

"Brother, if a segregationist like Johnson is now actively pushing for civil rights legislation, you have to know God is in charge," I said.

An echo of amen's resonated throughout the room. Lowery led us in a closing prayer and we all left reassured that this country was on the right track to eradicating segregation, and that President Johnson would be a better friend to the Negro than we had ever imagined.

In July 1964, the Civil Rights Act sailed through Congress. With Dr. King, Roy Wilkins of the NAACP and other dignitaries standing right behind him, President Johnson signed it into law. I watched the signing ceremony on the television in my office at the church. Once it was over, I got up and walked into the sanctuary. My thoughts were on Prof. Sims and Reverend Zimmerman. They were the prophets of their time, because they told us that our generation would carry the movement to another level. That was now a reality and I fell on my knees in front of the altar, clasped my hands together and thanked the Lord for his grace and kindness.

On Election Day in November 1964, Negroes overwhelmingly voted for Lyndon Johnson and he won re-election in a landslide victory. We now had a law that made any forms of segregation a federal offense and a president who was our friend. The Negro in the south had reason to rejoice. That year our Christmas was truly a blessed one because all of us, together, had received the greatest gift of all, and that was the gift of freedom.

21.

By 1965, Bethel was one of the fastest growing churches in Gaffney. The word was spreading that I was a very progressive minister who took his responsibility to preach the word of God seriously, while at the same time staying very active in the social change that was spreading throughout the south. Despite the subtle warning from the Union School Board, I never looked back as the civil rights fight continued to heat up all over the south. Ministers were in the lead role as they confronted obstacles to progress, but continued to fight on. Dr. King's house had been bombed as had Reverend Fred Shuttlesworth's home. Shuttlesworth had been beaten many times by Bull Connors's goons, but he just kept coming back for more, and the racist couldn't understand why.

In the past, violence had been the most effective intimidation factor, and it had worked. Now ministers were showing the way for the rest of the people. We all watched when Shuttlesworth stood outside his bombed home and told reporters that if God was on his side, there was nothing the racist could do to hamper his work. That became our motto throughout the south.

The worst that had happened to me was to be threatened by a school board. I felt blessed and refused to turn back. As we moved into the early spring months that year, the new battle lines were being drawn around voting rights for our people.

Word spread throughout the religious community that President Johnson was initially opposed to legislation supporting voting rights for the Negro in the South. He felt that it was too soon after passage of the 1964 Civil Rights Act to push congress for another Civil Rights Bill, and especially one that would give the Negro parity at the voting polls. Since passage of the Fifteenth Amendment as far back as 1870, whites had fought viciously to make sure the Negro could not vote. In fact, that was the initial impetus for the creation of the Ku Klux Klan. But Johnson's position soon reversed as a result of the incidents that occurred in Selma, Alabama in March of that year.

I sat in my office at the church watching a large contingent of marchers heading toward the Edmund Pettus Bridge in Selma. The marchers planned to cross the bridge and walk the fifty miles to Montgomery, Alabama for the purpose of challenging the voter registration laws in the state. Alabama Governor George Wallace had vowed to stop any protest that was aimed at challenging the legitimate laws of the state. He had called out the National Guard to prevent such an occurrence. The television cameras followed the marchers' movement up the street, and then switched over to catch the National Guard standing on the side of the road with riot gear on and nightsticks in their hands. It was obvious that they were ready to bust some heads wide open.

I recognized one of the leaders of the march. It was young John Lewis who helped organize the Student Non-Violent Coordinating Committee after the student sit-ins back in 1960. He had become one of the leading young voices in the movement and had spoken eloquently at the Lincoln Monument during the 1963 March on Washington D. C. The marchers seemed oblivious to the danger staring at them only a few yards away.

Suddenly pandemonium broke out. For some reason, the National Guard decided to strike out against the marchers. They began to attack them, even as they tried to retreat. The Guards wouldn't let them get away. With riot gear in full use they began to pound the marchers indiscriminately. One guard swung his club viciously at John Lewis, knocking him to the ground. I was stunned watching men and women beaten unmercifully. How could this be happening in America? The beatings lasted for about fifteen minutes but it seemed like it was fifteen years. I aged watching my friends and allies attacked in such a vicious manner.

Right at that moment my faith was tested. This was the perfect time for the devil, as he had done with Christ, to tempt me. But I rejected his temptation by rushing out of my office and into the sanctuary. As before, I fell on my knees and prayed. My hands trembled and sweat dripped down my forehead. But within minutes my anger subsided, as God touched me and reminded me that our Savior had suffered much more than any of us. And if He endured so could we, no matter how much the agents of the devil tortured our people. We were in a battle of good and evil and if we gave in the devil would win and the malicious forces of segregation would rule for another hundred years. The words of my ancestors echoed throughout my mind. They told me to "hold on just a little bit longer," as they had done in the past. They had brought us up the rough side of the mountain, and the work left to be done was minor compared to the work they did on our behalf. My resolve increased considerably after watching the massacre in Selma and then praying to my God, who sent me the word to keep fighting because change was on its way.

After the beatings at the Pettus Bridge, we received word from the SCLC that the president had changed his mind and was considering a voting rights bill. But first he asked Governor Wallace to visit him in the White House. Dr. King had planned another march from Selma to Montgomery and the president was determined to convince Wallace to call off his dogs. I had to call Malachi and talk with him. As soon as he picked up the phone, I got right to the point.

"Do you trust President Johnson?" I asked

"Trust him in what way?" Malachi replied. "What are you talking about? He delivered on the civil rights bill so I guess I have to say I trust him as much as you can trust a politician."

"I take it you haven't heard that he's planning on introducing legislation dealing with voting rights," I said.

"No, I hadn't heard. When did this happen?"

"Just this morning I got a message from SCLC. They wanted us to spread the word to all the ministers that Johnson will be meeting with George Wallace sometime next week. His goal is to convince him to call off his troops when Dr. King resumes the march from Selma to Montgomery. Once that is done, he's going to have the legislation introduced in the Senate."

"I guess you're asking me do I trust that he'll do what he says." Malachi asked rhetorically. "Based on how well he delivered in the civil rights bill last year, I guess I'll have to say that yes I do trust him. Don't you?"

"If Johnson does this it will be revolutionary. Do you know what that'll mean to Negroes throughout the south?" I asked, but did not wait for answer. "It means that Negroes will be able to elect mayors, congressmen, governors and even someday a president."

"Let's not get too carried away here," Malachi interjected. "We have to get the vote and then we're still a long way from electing a president. That won't happen until the next century and we'll be blessed to be alive if it does happen."

"I hear what you're saying and I agree. But if we get the vote here in South Carolina, there is an excellent chance we'll have someone in Congress within the next twenty years. President Johnson is beginning to be the best president for the Negro since Abraham Lincoln," I said.

"God is always right on time," Malachi said. "Let's pray that the president doesn't get removed by some maniac like what happened to Lincoln and Kennedy."

"Do you realize that we're living in the middle of some fascinating times in this country's history, and we are playing a role in these changes. God is using his ministers to make a change."

"When does Dr. King plan to march in Selma?"

"Next weekend."

"We have to pray that it all goes well. I worry about him. He's been getting all kinds of death threats."

"God will keep him here just as long as He needs him to do His work, and when King has done his job, he'll be rewarded."

"If we get this voting rights act, do you plan on running for office?" Malachi asked catching me somewhat off guard.

"Not at all," I said. "My work is in the church. My people need me for spiritual guidance and when possible I will offer my help to create social change, but running for office is not for me. How about you, Dunc, you ever plan on running for office? "

"Not a chance," Malachi replied. "I love the pulpit too much to get distracted by politics. But I will offer my support to some young man or woman who will surface as a leader in the state. I understand there is a young preacher Jesse Jackson who is becoming one of King's leading lieutenants and he's from South Carolina. I believe he went to South Carolina State."

"Yeah, I heard about him also," I said. " But he's kinda gone national. There is another young man out of South Carolina State. I believe his name is James Clyburn. I believe he's from Sumter, and has been involved in the student demonstrations down there. Looks like he might have a lot of potential."

"One thing we know is that we have a great deal of talent and it looks good for South Carolina in the future."

"We've had some great role models that went before us so what else would you expect?"

"You got that right. Listen I have to get over to the church."

"Let's pray that our president is successful one more time and soon we'll have a voting rights bill." We finished and I hung up the phone with a smile on my face. "Thank you Jesus," I prayed and then started for home.

Our prayers were again answered when on August 5, President Johnson signed the Voting Rights Bill into law. In just over a year the president had removed most vestiges of the old south, and we were dealing with a new day. But our schools were still segregated, and it was now time to force a change for the better. Time was running out for the school board, and there could be no more excuses. Integration of the schools was inevitable but it wouldn't happen unless we forced the issue.

Our goal for 1966 had to be desegregation of the schools, which would complete our fight for equality. I constantly thanked God for Jack Millwood and his determination to convince the school board and the biracial commission that it was time. And that happened early in 1966.

"James, I believe we have the necessary votes on the commission to bring about a mild form of integration in the fall,"

Jack said to me over the phone.

I gripped the phone tightly and stared out the window of the church office at a very light snow falling and melting as it hit the ground. It was rather strange for us to get snow in early March but maybe it was a sign of change. Certainly what Jack explained to me represented change, also. But I wondered what he meant by a mild form of integration.

"What do you think will work?" I asked

"I pooled the members of the commission to see how they felt about integrating Gaffney High School. As long we have a majority vote on our commission, I believe the school board will go along with our decision."

"Yes, but will the parents?" I asked, turning my attention from the snow to our conversation.

"If the school board goes along with it, then it's their job to convince the parents that this is something that has to be done," Jack said with some frustration in his tone. "My God Reverend, it has been over ten years since the court ruled in favor of de-segregation. If the court is going to retain any respectability, the south has to accept the decision and comply."

"You'll get no argument from me and my people. The burden of proof is on the shoulders of your people."

"I know and in many ways that frightens me. Why we want to hold on to the past, I don't know."

"I guess in their minds they feel their way is right," I said not wanting to sound too harsh, since it seemed as though the issue of integrating the schools might be breaking in our favor. "The mayor has placed you in a very difficult situation. You have to convince your people that the system they believed in all these years was wrong. And a people they felt were their inferior are indeed equal to them, and deserve to be treated as such. Good luck my friend." I finished and we hung up the phone.

Jack did pool the commission after much debate and they decided to adopt a compromise position. Instead of moving forward with a forced desegregation, they decided to implement a freedom of choice policy. The plan allowed parents to choose what school within the district they wanted their children to attend. We knew that most of the white parents would reject the idea, but just possibly we could convince some Black parents to go along with it, and at least get the process of integration started. To my surprise an overwhelming majority of Black parents also opposed the idea.

One evening I invited the parents to attend a meeting at Bethel to discuss the possibility of breaking down segregation by sending their children to white schools. The church was packed to the point that people were standing out in the vestibule leading into the church. I had never before experienced the community so adamant against a plan to integrate.

"Rev, we respect you and know you trying to do your best to change things, but I just don't want my kids exposed to all that violence and people calling them nigger," one of the attendees said.

"Yeah, Rev, we remember what happened at Central High School in Little Rock. Those white people acted a fool," a lady who was a member of my church concurred.

"But how we going to bring about change unless we make the necessary sacrifices. Those boys and girls in Raleigh been called every name in the book and actually been beat up, but they fought on until a new movement got started. If they had taken that attitude we wouldn't be as far advanced as we are now," I said.

"We got no right to jeopardize the safety of our children for some kind of cause," a man in the back of the church shouted. "Why don't them white folks bring their children down here to our schools. Why we always got to go to them?"

"Because we are the stronger people and just because they won't do right, doesn't mean we shouldn't," I said. I was getting irritated, but didn't want to let them know.

"My kids ain't going nowhere less some of their kids come up here," another man shouted. "Our schools just as good as theirs and our teachers just as good too. If they can't come to us we ain't going to them."

"People, it's not about who is good or who is bad, it is about change," I now shouted. "We need change if this country is going to be a better place for all of us to live. Dr. King and those young folks have shown us the way, now we have to follow."

"I ain't following nobody nowhere when my children's safety is at stake. Them white folks is fools and they is crazy and they ain't never liked no Negroes," another woman shouted.

"If the plan is approved by the School Board, my children are going to integrate West End Elementary School in the fall because it is only two blocks from where we live, and it never made any sense for them not to be going there," I said emphatically. "Now is there any other parents willing to join me."

One of my deacons at the church stood and said. "My son will join your children, Reverend."

"Thank you Brother," I said. "Anyone else?"

A man from Limestone Church also stood. "We'll send our children also," he said.

"As long as you willing to do it, Reverend, we'll send our two children over to West End," a man, with his wife stood up and said. "We trust in your leadership and we got to support you in order to get these things done."

"Thank you Brother, " I said. "Anyone else?" None of the others in the audience stood. They folded their arms as they sat and fought change.

"Good," I said. "I will let the commission know that we do have some children willing to integrate West End."

As the summer progressed, I had two additional families join us. We had about twelve young people who would begin the process of integrating the Cherokee County School System in the fall of 1966, and that was a good start.

22.

I always found it an interesting argument from lay people outside the church, that a preacher's children spend too much time at church and as a result rebel when they get older. Rubye and I never bought into that kind of thinking. For as far as I was concerned, there was no better place for children than in the church. If a place of worship is not the right environment for young children, then I'd like to know what is the alternative?

Since I was a minister at two different churches, Bethel in Gaffney and the other Bethel in Kelton. Jewette, James, Jr., and Russlyn all knew they would be attending services at both places. As children and young adults, until they moved out of our home, they were required to attend Sunday school, morning service, and an evening service at Bethel. And those times that Rubye went to Bethel in Kelton, they went with us.

They also had to attend bible study every Wednesday evening. Bible study was as important as Sunday service. The true and dedicated believers were the members who came to Bible study. For many of my members Sunday service was more of a social gathering; a time and place to show off a new dress or suit, and a chance to drive up and park in the church parking lot in a recently purchased new car. But Bible study on Wednesday was no frills, and dedicated to studying the Lord's word. It was mandatory that my entire family be there to meet and greet the members who showed up that evening.

That caused problems when the South Carolina State Fair was in Spartanburg. Wednesday had traditionally been the day that Black people from Gaffney went to the fair, and it was always in the evening. Since we had prayer meeting on Wednesday, I would take the children out there in the morning and we would leave by six o'clock. Even though they never expressed displeasure, I know they hated having to leave before their friends got there later that evening. But no matter the occasion or the event, it was mandatory that we all be in church on Wednesday evening for prayer meeting.

My children were also required to sing in the children's choir every third Sunday. They also participated in church programs on Christmas and Easter. Jewette, who had become quite an accomplished pianist, played a couple of melodies on the old piano in the church. James Jr., and Ruzlin recited verses from the Bible or a poem relevant to the holiday we were celebrating.

Rubye and I did our best to keep our children grounded in reality. We constantly preached to them how blessed they were, but never to think they were better than anyone else. However, one time I believe Rubye carried that lesson a little too far.

Jewette, James, Jr. and Ruzlin were curious about cotton. We would often drive along the highway and they saw the sharecroppers out in the fields picking cotton. We explained to them that our history was filled with years of working in the cotton fields, and how Prof. Sims told parents if they gave him their kids for four years in school, they would never pick cotton again. I used Nette, Grady and me as examples of what education could do for you. All three of us had graduated from college and both Nette and Grady were teaching school in the Washington, D.C. area. But they were still curious about the cotton fields, since many of their friends were forced to work the fields in the summer.

One afternoon I came home early and the children were gone. I asked Rubye where they were and to my surprise, she told me that she had taken them out into the country, and signed them up to pick cotton.

"You did what?" I shouted.

"Took them out to experience picking cotton," she repeated.

"I don't want my kids picking cotton or working in the cotton fields."

"Rev, they told me they wanted to join some of their friends and work with them," she said.

I snatched my car keys and headed for the door.

"What field did you take them to?" I scowled.

"The Carlisle Farm."

"I'm going to get my kids."

"But Rev, they'll probably be way out in the field. It's only noon."

"Don't care. I'm getting my children. You coming?"

Rubye jumped in the passenger seat and I drove out to the farm. When we got there, the workers were well out in the field, but our three children sat out front of the farmhouse. They looked tired and disheveled. When they saw us, their faces lit up. All three of them jumped into the back seat of the car, and before we were back on the highway they were asleep. Evidently, they couldn't take the hot sun, the weeds and bending over all the time. They just quit and returned to the front of the farm. They worked long enough to make ten cents each. They never asked to pick cotton again.

In February 1968, the US District Court ruled the choice plan for integrating the schools unconstitutional. It was rejected because it didn't work. Only a few Negro parents chose schools other than the black ones, and none of the white population sent their children to Negro schools. The city was required to implement a busing plan by the fall of 1968.

Jack knew there would be trouble from the white parents if their children were required to attend Granard. We talked about the potential violence that surrounded and threatened Little Rock, Arkansas back in 1957. Gaffney had managed to stay beneath the radar of racial violence that was endemic in southern cities. We had to come up with a plan to circumvent trouble, and the best way to do that was to close Granard and transfer all its students to Gaffney. Instead of busing white students, we decided to bus the Negroes. The Negro parents were not happy with the plan, but there was nothing else we could do. Gaffney had to come into compliance with the Court Order, and even though I didn't like the plan, it was the best we could do at the time. We could only pray that in the fall it would all go smoothly, without any major problems. We were hopeful that the plan would work and we could maintain harmony among the races. However, two events occurred within the next three months that threatened the continued peace in the south and in Gaffney.

The first incident was in Orangeburg, South Carolina at the All Star Bowling Alley. Negro students from nearby South Carolina State decided to picket the bowling alley because the owners refused to comply with the Civil Rights Act of 1964, and allow Negroes to bowl. Two hundred students picketed in front of the facility, and the irate owners called the police. After an exchange of words between the police and the students one of the trigger-happy policemen fired into the crowd. Before the smoke had cleared three young men were killed and twenty-eight wounded.

That unprovoked attack by the police on innocent and unarmed students, sent tremors throughout the community. Negroes were ready to take up arms and retaliate. The ministers were called on to maintain peace. The city leaders in Gaffney asked for a meeting with our ministers' alliance. We met with them and promised we would talk with our congregations. I was beginning to feel like an appeaser for white violence against our people. But for us there was no other choice. Violence was not an alternative, because in the long run we were terribly out manned and out gunned. If we adopted a policy to strike back with force, the outcome would be disastrous, and I was certain that many whites would love for that to happen. We were able to calm the waters in Gaffney among the young ones who sought revenge, but we weren't sure how many times we could take on this role and be successful.

Two months later we were confronted with another possible disastrous situation, as was the entire country when Dr. Martin Luther King, Jr., was assassinated in Memphis, Tennessee. That one act represented another test of King's non-violent approach as the model for justice and equality for our people. As ministers we had accepted that approach because we knew it was in keeping with the teachings of Christ. But how could we continue to preach non-violence to our followers when white Southerners constantly killed, lynched, and maimed Blacks throughout the south.

The Life of Reverend James W. Sanders

Our association did the best it could to make sure there were no violent reactions in Gaffney and surrounding areas to the King murder. We watched and read in shock, the number of riots that broke out up north and even in the nation's capitol. With the help of ministers like C.V. Owens and others we maintained a peace in Gaffney, even though we felt the same anger as others over King's death.

In a frank and open meeting with the white leaders of the city, we let them know that at some point they would have to convince their people to follow our example. They couldn't expect us to continuously preach non-violence when our people were the victims of white aggression. Blacks were no longer fearful of whites as they had been in the past. We reminded them that the younger Negroes preached a different approach based on Black Power and, as much as we opposed that method, they would ultimately win out if white leadership could not stop the violence. We pointed out that the murder of Emmit Till, Medgar Evars, the four little girls and two boys in Birmingham, Alabama, the three civil rights workers in Mississippi, Viola Luouza, the three students in Orangeburg, and now Dr. King had to stop. And most important, if they continued to kill then at some point justice had to be served, and these murderers must be tried and convicted in a fair and equitable court of law.

Out of respect for Dr. King a contingent of South Carolina ministers, to include Reverend Zimmerman, Malachi and I traveled to Atlanta to attend his funeral. It was a very solemn and disturbing atmosphere in Atlanta. We had lost a hero, a leader and a man of God to evil, and it was difficult to maintain positive feelings on that day. There were two funerals that day. The first was at Ebenezer Baptist Church where he was pastor. That was for family and close friends only. The second was at Morehouse College and was open to the public. It was preceded by a poor people's march from Ebenezer to the campus of the college. We joined in that march.

The auditorium at Morehouse College was packed and we were forced to watch the service on a television in one of the adjoining rooms. We were proud that a fellow South Carolinian, Dr. Benjamin Mays, preached the eulogy. Mays was representative of the great South Carolina ministers, such as Reverend A. C. Duncan and Reverend Zimmerman. He preached one of the best sermons in his long stellar career.

"The tragedy of life doesn't lie in not reaching your goal," he said. "The tragedy lies in having no goal to reach. It isn't a calamity to die with dreams unfulfilled. But it is a calamity not to dream."

Those words best personified the life of Dr. King. They were the same words that Dr. Mays had spoken in the past to many students who studied under him, to include Dr. King. To repeat them at the funeral was especially appropriate, because they also reflected the vision we all had of King when he talked of his dream at the 1963 March on Washington, D.C. They gave us hope for the future and a strong determination to continue down the path that King had established over the past fifteen years.

The King murder and the stirring eulogy delivered that April day by Dr. Mays inspired me to continue my battle against the forces of racial bias. I would not rest until all vestiges of an anachronistic system of evil were wiped from the face of the earth. I could do my share in Gaffney to make that happen.

In the fall of 1968, the school board began bussing children to Gaffney High School and they closed Granard High. It had served Black children since 1901 and many of the parents opposed the move but we had no choice. There was no way we could expect a peaceful transition if we attempted to send white students to Granard. So we sent our Black children to Gaffney High School. James, Jr., and Ruzlin graduated from Gaffney. The change was pretty much problem free and we were able to integrate faster than other surrounding cities like Spartanburg.

One of the major problems we confronted was the transfer of teachers from Granard to Gaffney. Very few Black teachers were hired with the change. I knew this would be a problem with the Cherokee County School Board of Education. They were not comfortable with the idea of Black teachers instructing white children. In order to overcome their opposition we would need a large contingent of Black parents to show up at the Board meeting when I planned to confront the Board members. Immediately, I recognized that as a job for the Ministerial Alliances.

The week before the meeting I notified all the ministers in

the Cherokee County Black Ministerial Alliance and those in the Thickety Mountain Baptist Association to encourage their congregations to be at that meeting. It worked perfectly. The evening of the Board meeting over one thousand Blacks showed up. There weren't enough seats in the chamber to accommodate all the people and they were over flowing out into the hallway. With their support I was able to present our position and win. The Board agreed to hire at least five Black teachers that first year and it would increase over the years. Gaffney had finally integrated its schools and without any violence. The biracial commission, the school board and the city officials all worked well together and we did what a lot of the south was unable to do and that is a peaceful integration of the schools.

Another positive development was the commitment of the National Association for the Advancement of Colored People to accept social protest as a legitimate tool for change. There was reconciliation between the followers of King who believed change was possible through peaceful protest and the NAACP who for years depended only on legal channels to achieve equality. I believe all sides finally decided that we could achieve our goals by working together. We continued our active participation through protest while the organization remained focused on challenging bad and unjust laws in the courts. We all agreed that protest through boycott was an acceptable method to achieve change. That kind of cooperation was the foundation behind our joint effort to wipe out any form of segregation in Gaffney.

In a cooperative effort with the NAACP we integrated the Cherokee Theater, we eliminated that law forcing Blacks to sit in the balcony at the Hambrick, and we integrated the Laundromat that had years ago refused to allow me to wash clothes there. Slowly all vestiges of segregation were falling so that by 1970 integration was complete in our city. We were aware that racism was still alive but at least we had removed it as an obstacle to our liberties.

That racism raised its ugly head when a group of white citizens, Sons of the Confederacy, asked the city council to fly the Confederate flag over the municipal building. I viewed that as a direct slap in the face of the Blacks living in Gaffney and immediately organized the ministers to march on city hall.

During the city council meeting the Sons of the Confederacy spoke in favor of flying the flag as part of their heritage and in honor of their ancestors who had died defending states rights and freedom for the South to live their lives as they saw fit. I followed them and countered with the argument that the flag, while acknowledging one group's heritage dismissed other citizens of the city, who found the flag offensive and a reminder of the ugly past that still haunted the south. I also stressed the fact that the Civil War was not fought for states rights but for denial of rights of freedom for four million men and women caught in the ugly system of slavery.

The city council voted overwhelmingly not to fly the flag. I viewed that as a victory for all of the citizens seeking a fair and equitable relationship among the races in the South and especially in Gaffney. With that victory and the many other victories we had experienced over the years, my position as leader in Gaffney was set in stone and would remain so for many years to come.

In the summer of 1970, Union, South Carolina finally implemented a school desegregation policy and Sims High School was caught right in the middle of it. White children were scheduled to be bussed to Sims, and along with the children came a number of white teachers. For obviously racial reasons, the school board assigned a white administrator as the new principal over me. I had been at Sims since 1953 and was not going to passively sit around a let them abuse me in that manner.

The only protest I could make was to quit and that is what I did. I knew it was time for me to move on and give my full attention to Bethel and the struggle for equal rights. I was the one minister in the Gaffney area who had a large enough congregation that I could depend on them for a decent salary. That meant I was not forced to back down to any race issue that needed leadership from someone not dependent on whites for survival. Most of the local ministers did not have congregations large enough to pay them a salary that would allow them the opportunity to do nothing but pastor their church. They all had other jobs and were subject to being fired if they took a position not supported by their employer.

I had assumed many leadership roles in the community, but now free of the responsibility associated with being Vice

Principal at Sims, I was able to take on more issues important to my community in Gaffney. I was the one individual that both Black and whites turned to if there was any kind of racial crisis that needed to be adjudicated.

Such a crisis occurred at the beginning of the school year in 1970 when two Black students were expelled from Gaffney High School. The other Blacks felt that the expulsion was unfair and threatened to walk out the next day. The school called Jack who then called me.

"James, we have a potentially explosive situation at the high school," he said.

"What's going on?" I asked

"Seems as though two Negro students were kicked out of school and now all the others are threatening to walk out tomorrow. James, you have to know that would be a disastrous move on their part."

"I know what you mean," I said. "All the critics of integration would use it as a reason to declare integration a failure."

"You're exactly right. I heard that the mayor is considering sending the police in to make sure that they don't leave. That would make the national news and we don't need that kind of publicity. Our integration has gone quite well so far. Can you do something about this?"

"With God's grace and some sensible thinking parents, I'll do my best." We hung up and I immediately made calls to ministers throughout the city. They also agreed that would be a disastrous situation, and agreed to make announcements from the pulpits to their members who had students at Gaffney High.

The ministers convinced their members who had children at Gaffney High School to discuss this matter with them. The parents were able to talk their children out of boycotting the classes. The issue of the two suspended students was resolved when I met with the Principal at Gaffney High and order was restored to what could have had a tragic ending.

23.

The gubernatorial election in the fall of 1970 was a testament to the changing political and social environment in South Carolina. It was an articulation of the new breed of white leadership taking on the old guard. There was a large contingent of whites who recognized that they had to make adjustments to meet the needs of the new south. Segregation was becoming a drain on the financial resources of the business community. Industries such as tourism were hurting because visitors from other parts of the country refused to come south because of the possibility of violence and in protest against the apartheid system of government. As a result, the business community began to shift their position and reluctantly supported integration of all the facilities.

There was also a group of progressive whites who opposed the old way simply because it was both ethically and morally wrong. They were outraged over the Orangeburg incident and especially the fact that no one was punished for those murders. These men and women were determined to change the image of the Democratic Party. Their leader was John West, the Lieutenant Governor who while in the legislature had voted against bills that would have closed integrated colleges, and legislation designed to keep other facilities segregated, regardless of the Civil Rights Act of 1964. He easily won the Democratic Party's nomination for governor and the Black ministers in the state rallied behind his candidacy.

Considering the political position of West's opponent, it was easy for us to support him. Albert Watson was the incumbent Congressmen from the 2nd Congressional District, which covered the Central Eastern part of the state to include Columbia, the state's capitol. Watson's district was of historical importance to Black South Carolinians. That seat was held by Jacob Ransier, a Black man, for one time in 1873, and then again by Robert H. Cain from 1875 to 1879. But with the collapse of the Reconstruction Period and the advent of Jim Crow Laws, no Black had been elected from that district or any other congressional district since Cain. It was, however, the prime target for a future Black congressman given its large Negro population.

Congressman Watson ran originally as a Democrat, but after passage of the 1964 Civil Rights Act and the 1965 Voting Rights Bill, he switched parties as did many of the elected officials throughout the south. Many of the politicians in South Carolina followed their leader, Strom Thurmond, who switched parties in the early 1960's. Their catalyst for change was that President Johnson had double-crossed his southern buddies when he staunchly supported civil rights legislation. It was the beginning of a trend that would continue for years.

Since passage of the Voting Rights Bill, the ministers in the state had made registering to vote a high priority. I insisted that all my members register. Most of them did and were definitely ready to cast their vote, many for the very first time in the Governor's race. Because of the vitriolic rhetoric Watson was slinging at integration, we knew it was mandatory that we help to defeat him. I was irate when we learned that some of his white supporters had attacked and turned over a school bus full of Negro children, after one of his hate filled speeches. At that point I was determined that he would never become governor.

In October I invited West to speak at Bethel. It really wasn't necessary because I already knew my congregation would be voting for him. But he came and spoke. After his speech, I asked that if he won, would he appoint a Negro to his staff. He gave me his word, and I took note to remind him of that promise after the election.

The election was extremely close but West did win. It was the first time in the history of the state that a winning candidate garnered more votes from Blacks than he did from whites. The Voting Rights Act had made all the difference and from that point on, the Negro population would be a constituency politicians would have to contend with in the future.

The Life of Reverend James W. Sanders

I drove up to Columbia for West's swearing-in ceremony. We stood outside the Capitol and listened to this man speak words that I never thought I would hear from a white Governor in the state of South Carolina. West vowed to rid the state government of any vestiges of discrimination. He promised a color-blind administration. My God, I thought, we as Black people were making progress toward equality. It was just so unfortunate that men like Prof. Sims, Mr. Williams, and other leading voices of the 1940's who instructed us to keep fighting for change never had the opportunity to hear a governor of this state talk in such a manner. And it was also unfortunate that they weren't around to witness the first Black to work at the highest echelons of the state government.

Immediately after West was sworn in. a delegation of ministers and leaders of the state, met with him. At that time we reminded him of his promise and he kept it. He named a young, bright, up-coming leader of the community to his staff. James Clyburn from Sumner was one of the brightest and political savvy men in the state. Young Clyburn was the product of a strong Black family and had leadership qualities written all over him. His father was a minister, who spoke out for civil rights as did his mother who owned her own beauty salon.

Clyburn had participated in a number of the civil rights marches and demonstrations while a student at South Carolina State in Orangeburg. He was arrested in 1961 for participating in a protest march at the South Carolina State Capitol. He was also leader of the Student Non-violent Coordinating Committee on campus. Both the ministerial and lay leaders supported him for the position.

West did not stop with just a political appointment to his staff. In 1974 he created the Human Rights Commission with the purpose of researching the Orangeburg killings of 1968. The goal of the commission was to assure that such tragedies never occurred again. He also named Clyburn as the Commissioner to oversee the new agency's operation. He would remain in that position for eighteen years before launching a historical campaign for congress. During those years I met with him often to discuss policies that could improve the relationship between whites and Blacks in the state. Clyburn was so astute at his job he served in that position through the administrations of two Democratic and two Republican governors.

Governor West's defeat of Strom Thurmond's handpicked candidate seemed to have an effect on how the long-time racist viewed the changing political climate in the state. He began to soften his position on civil rights issues. He reached out more to his Black constituents. He began calling me, and seeking my advice on a number of issues. I even allowed him to speak at my church, for which I received severe criticism from leaders in the civil rights movement. My feeling, however, was one of healing. As a minister it was my appointed duty to resolve issues of hatred with love, a policy that Dr. King always preached. One of the great attributes of our race is the ability to forgive. When I witnessed Dr. King deliver a sermon based on forgiveness at the Sixteenth Street Baptist Church in September 1963, I was more than convinced that we all must find the same kind of strength to forgive, as the walls of segregation began to crumble.

In the summer of 1976, Senator Thurmond invited James, Jr., to serve as an intern for a year in his office. James jumped at the opportunity to work in a Senator's office. He lived with his Uncle Grady who had relocated to Washington when he finished college. I didn't feel that this was an opportunity my son should pass up even though he was in the office of a Republican. I viewed this as another indication of Thurmond's evolving attitude about race. Finally, I encouraged Thurmond to support the King Holiday Legislation, which he initially opposed. But his opposition was based on cost, and once it was proven by the Congressional Budget Office that it was more financially beneficial to have the holiday than not to, he changed his mind and voted for passage. Who would have thought that the staunchest racist in the country back in the pre-civil rights days, would ever vote to create a holiday for a man that he considered his enemy, for years. There was no doubt that we were making progress toward racial equality in the south, and in South Carolina.

By the middle of the 1970's, Bethel had also become one of the largest and most progressive churches in the city. From my inception as the minister there, I had made it a goal to build a church for all ages, from the elderly to the young. We had programs to serve all groups. Bethel had the only Kindergarten school in Gaffney.

It was necessary since many of the mothers in our congregation worked, and they needed a place for their children during the day. While the children were with us, our teachers instructed them in reading, writing and their numbers and also instilled race pride in who they were. The children that went through our program were well prepared for when they entered elementary school

I also implemented a summer employment program for our youth. The church entered into a relationship with many of the businesses in the community. They provided our young adults with jobs and we paid their salary, with the majority of their money going into two-thousand dollar scholarships for college. They were also required to tithe ten percent of the salary to the church. Parents in and around Gaffney were so impressed with our progressive programs they were flocking to our church.

The church trustees and deacons also agreed to implement an interest free loan program for the members. They could borrow what they were able to re-pay, according to their monthly salary. We allowed the members borrowing the money to set the amount they could re-pay on a monthly basis. But we would use their home or land as collateral for the loan, and just as the bank would do, we would call in the loan if they refused to pay it back. If necessary we would foreclose on their property. It was not something we enjoyed doing but we had to do it if the member refused to pay the loan. There were a number of members who did lose their property to the church. But for the most part, the majority of the members who took out the loans paid them back.

The frailty of our lives is never questioned until we are forced to confront the reality of death. In 1978, that reality came crashing down on me when Mama got sick and in August of that year passed away. Her homegoing service was held at the church where she had been a member since before I was born, Corinth in Union. I asked and Poppa concurred that the Reverend A. C. Duncan conduct her service. He did and it was beautiful. Like most sons feel about their mother, I mourned her death. But joy comes in the morning when you know your loved one was saved, believed in Jesus Christ as their savior and loved the Lord. Mama was there in Heaven preparing that mansion and just waiting on Poppa.

The next year Poppa made that trip to the other side of the river and joined his wife in their mansion in the sky. He died in April 1979, less than a year after Mama. I knew that had to be a planned exit. Two people who were so in love and compatible have to be rejoined for eternity. This time Reverend Zimmerman preached his home going service. Having been a trustee of the church for so many years, the members gave him a no strings barred good bye. I knew that for a long time Christmas morning would not be the same, because we would no longer have our special breakfast with Mama and Poppa. I also recognized that my role was now as the senior man in the family. It was my turn to assume the mantle of leadership for the Sanders' family. At the age of fifty, I occupied the role that Grandpa had held for so many years and Poppa for the past ten.

In June 1985 I received news that Grady was diagnosed with cancer. By the time he made it to the doctor the cancer was already in Stage 4. I prayed everyday after that for the Lord to cure him, but this was one prayer that would not be answered in the positive. By December of that same year, we got word to make it up to Washington, D.C. because Grady had passed. I was crushed and wasn't sure I could attend his home going ceremony. But I quickly came to my senses. Grady was out of his misery and was home with the Lord. It was all right to mourn his loss, but again joy comes in the morning. My faith told me to be strong, drive up to Washington with my family and give my brother the proper send off he deserved. That is exactly what we did. The entire family attended the service at the church where Grady had been a deacon for years, Bethel Baptist. After the service I felt a satisfactory degree of closure. I had honored my brother's memory, assisted in laying him to rest and put it all in the hands of God. I was confident that I would see my brother once again on the other side of the river.

By the end of 1980 we had one of the largest congregations in Gaffney. Over six hundred members for a city the size of Gaffney was quite an accomplishment. In 1989, we launched a four-year project designed to build a new and modern sanctuary with a family life center and a fully equipped gymnasium. And by 1991, the project was complete and the new facilities were functional. It cost us approximately 1.1 million dollars, all raised from donations from the congregation.

The Life of Reverend James W. Sanders

It made me feel good that all three of my children had returned to Bethel to work in the church, after attending college out of state. Jewette went to Barber Scotia College in Concord, North Carolina, Ruzlin attended Spelman in Atlanta and James, Jr. went to Morehouse College, also in Atlanta and then attended South Carolina Law School for one year. He finally settled on the ministry, and after graduating from divinity school returned to Bethel to be an assistant pastor. Jewette had played the piano for the choir throughout high school and assumed that position once she returned from college. After attending Spelman for one year, Ruzlin returned to Gaffney and finished at Limestone College. She became secretary and treasurer for the church.

My children have a tremendous passion for Bethel. They grew up spending many weekdays and every Sunday all day between its walls. But most important they have great love for the Lord. Rubye and I did our job as parents. We delivered all three of our children to God, and they will always remain loyal to Him.

Because of the success I enjoyed at Bethel, other churches in the state of South Carolina and as far away as Washington, D.C. sought me out. One of those churches was Macedonia Baptist in Washington, D.C. They invited me to come up and preach one Sunday and within a week offered me the job to become their pastor. It was a tempting offer because both Nette and Grady were living in the Washington, D.C. area and I did miss them. But Rubye, the kids, and my congregation were adamantly opposed to me leaving. It was Deacon James Ruff who put it to me succinctly. He told me that God had sent me to Bethel and that is where he meant for me to stay. His words were true, and my future was right there with the people I dearly loved and admired. God made my decision for me, through the words delivered by Deacon Ruff.

Over the years, I served as pastor of smaller churches in two Gaffney surrounding communities. For twenty-five years, I was pastor at Seatwell Baptist Church in Newberry, South Carolina. It was a small country church that held service on the first and third Sundays of the month. I accepted that position after Bethel in Kelton hired a full time pastor. I had promised Bethel in Gaffney that I would never accept a position that interfered with my duties to them. That is why I left Bethel in Kelton but accepted the position at Seatwell. I was also pastor of Island Creek Baptist Church in Cowpen. I accepted that position again under the same conditions that I had with the church in Kelton. Seatwell needed a full time every Sunday pastor and that interfered with my primary church duties. Island Creek was only every other Sunday. It was a fifteen-minute drive from Gaffney. I would drive down there for a nine o'clock service and be back to Bethel in time for the regular eleven o'clock service.

24.

As the walls of segregation continued to crumble, windows of opportunity for Blacks grew. One of the most important windows of opportunity came when the United States Supreme Court mandated that Congressional District Six in the state should be re-structured to advantage the election of a Black representative. As a result, the state legislature re-drew the boundary lines to include Black enclaves from the cities of Florence, Sumner, a large portion of Columbia and parts of Charleston. Recognizing the handwriting on the wall, Congressman Robin Tallon, whose district was most impacted by the re-drawing of the boundary lines, decided to call it quits. Five Blacks from the district, to include James Clyburn, threw their hats in the ring. Finally, after almost one hundred years, Blacks would elect one of their own to represent them in Congress.

Despite the fact that 1992 was a presidential election year and a young governor from Arkansas, Bill Clinton, appeared to be on the verge of a major upset against the incumbent George Bush, the congressional district race got all the buzz from the Black communities in the state. It was the logical first step toward political empowerment at the national level for Black South Carolinians. Even though it was only one congressional seat, the race carried greater implications for the future for all Blacks throughout the state.

Our ministerial alliances throughout the state unanimously supported James Clyburn, who had not only served on Governor West's staff, but also served on the Human Affairs Commission. He easily became the prohibitive favorite to win in the Democratic

213

primary, which was pretty much tantamount to winning the election. Because the 1965 Voting Rights Act was viewed as the work of progressive Democrats on Capitol Hill as well as President Johnson, when Blacks registered they automatically declared their loyalty to the Democratic Party. And many who had been Republicans over the years because of Abraham Lincoln, now switched over to the Democratic Party. Even though Gaffney was not in the Sixth Congressional District, our Ministerial Alliance let it be known that we supported James Clyburn and encouraged our congregation to contact relatives in the Sixth and suggest that they vote for him.

On Election Day, Clyburn registered over 55% of the vote in the primary. Because he garnered over 50%, there would be no run-off and he was now the first Black man to represent South Carolina in Congress since his great-great uncle George Washington Murray did from 1893 to 1897. Poetic justice prevailed and even though Murray was a Republican, it was fitting that one of his relatives one hundred years later, take his place in Congress.

Windows of opportunity began to open for me also. Many boards and commissions within the state sought me out to serve as one of their directors. In 1992, I received an appointment to the Appalachian Council of Governments. The Council represented six counties in South Carolina and set public policy over its jurisdictions. From 1996 to 1998, I was Chair of the Council and also served as Chair of the Advisory Committee to the Council.

Over the many years of struggle for equality, the Baptist ministers put their confidence in me as their leader, having re-elected me as Moderator of the Thickety Mountain Baptist Association for over thirty-eight years. When I assumed the mantle of leadership, I did it on the shoulders of a giant of a man, Reverend A.C. Duncan, the very man who had led my ordination into the ministry. I was also appointed a Trustee of Morris College and was awarded a Doctorate of Divinity from that school. I had already received a Master of Science from South Carolina A and T College in Greensboro, South Carolina.

A few years later I was appointed Second Vice Chair of the Trustee Board at South Carolina State University. In 2003, Governor Mark Sanford appointed me to fill an unexpired term on the Santee Cooper Board of Directors for the Fifth Congressional District in the state of South Carolina. Santee Cooper, also known as the South Carolina Public Authority, monitors usage of electricity and water utilities in the state. I took my appointment serious, and was active on many committees to include the Executive-Corporate Planning Committee, the Audit Committee, the Customer Relations Committee, the Property Committee and finally the Human Resources Committee. Even at my age, I am still very active on the Board. In 2008, the Governor re- appointed me to a full term on the Board.

Congressman John Spratt, who became Chair of the powerful Budget Committee in the United States House of Representatives, was a very close friend. He visited my church on numerous occasions. Whenever he needed advice on any legislation dealing with Blacks and the poor, he called me. The Cherokee Democratic Party also elected me as Vice-Chairman because of the influence I carried in the Black community.

My greatest honor, however, was that my son, James Jr., and Grady's two sons, Grady Jr. and Charles all became ministers. I was proud because the Sanders' name would continue the tradition I started when I committed to the ministry at fifteen, and ministered my first church while still in high school back in 1947. My son was right here at Bethel and my two nephews pastored churches in Washington, D. C. and Maryland.

I felt extremely blessed when I received an invitation in 2009 to the inauguration of the newly elect President of the United States, the Honorable Barack Obama. Even though I supported Hillary Clinton in the Democratic Primary, he overlooked that fact and reached out to me. As a child of the post-civil rights era, I am certain that he understood why many of us old warriors did not believe this country would actually elect a Black man to the highest office in this country. We had experienced great strides in civil rights but still had to acknowledge the historical fact that whites have always and for a long time into the future would continue to run this country. We sincerely believed that the only chance a Democrat had at winning was through the candidacy of Mrs. Clinton. She was a seasoned veteran, having gone through two presidential and three gubernatorial campaigns with her husband. It was important that the Republican candidate be defeated because we had suffered through eight terrible years of the Bush administration. For that reason we threw our support behind the white woman, instead of the Black man. It would be the one decision that we all would live to regret. We did, however, support Obama in the general election against the Republican candidate John McCain. And I felt proud and honored to be there to witness his swearing in ceremony.

That January day was extremely cold with a strong wind blowing in from the west. Rubye and I had arrived in the nation's capitol by plane the previous day and spent the night with my childhood friend and Latta's sister, Agnes Bright. She lived in Silver Spring, Maryland, a suburb of the capitol. While there I also had the opportunity to visit Matthew Zimmerman, who was now a retired Colonel in the United States Army and the Pastor of a Baptist church in Alexandria, Virginia. Matthew had done quite well for himself and was just another example of the fine men that came out of Union, South Carolina. We talked about those days when we all would go fishing and have our legs hanging over the bridge above the Broad River.

"I always admired you," Matthew said as we sat in the den of his home sipping on a hot cup of cocoa after a wonderful meal prepared by his wife.

"Those were tough days for Black folks, but they were days I don't think I would replace at all," I said.

"We all knew and especially Dad, that you would grow to be a leader, but we always thought it would be in Union."

"For some reason I felt that you would take a different direction in life and not become a minister."

"Are you kidding," Matthew smiled and crossed his legs. He sat in his big recliner near the fireplace that was heating the room from the logs that burned inside. "There was no way I could grow up in my Daddy's house and not follow him into the ministry. That was his ultimate dream. He trained so many other young ministers I couldn't deny him the pleasure of training his son also. And it has turned out to be quite a good profession."

I took another sip from my drink. It was hot and made an old man feel warm and good inside. I looked around the room. One wall was covered with beautiful bookshelves filled with all kinds of books and especially those that were about the military and ministry. The other wall had plagues, awards, and honors he had received while in the military. A few of them were honors he earned as a minister.

"All your awards indicate the success you have enjoyed and I know if your father was still living he would be exceptionally proud of you."

"As he would be of you also," Matthew rejoined. "Tomorrow you will have a front seat view of the swearing in of the first African American president in the history of this country. That's pretty heavy stuff."

"Yes it is and can you believe it took the young people to make us realize that what we never believed could happen, did. Our generation had been too beaten and somewhat broken over the years to believe that this white man would ever allow a Black to occupy the White House."

"At some point, we all have to move over. Someday those young folks who are about to replace us will have someone to replace them. Age slows down for no one. That's one thing that is an equal opportunity phenomenon, controlled only by God.

"You're right about that. It shows you exactly what God thinks of color. He makes sure all races do that one thing with each other. Let's pray that these young people have the sense to always put God first." I ran my fingers along the opening on top of the coffee cup. "Do you have any idea of how many good men are now locked up in prison and will never have the opportunity to dream of running for president. The streets kill the spirit and destroy the will to dream."

Matthew leaned forward in his chair. "I have a very difficult time accepting the negative and nihilistic attitude of these young people, even though I understand some of it may be justified. But they really do have it much easier than we did when the doors were blocked to us because of racism. Today someone may be a racist but he is unable to use his prejudice to prevent a Black or any boy of color from achieving his dream."

"At least tomorrow we can celebrate with the inauguration of President Obama. We've come a long way and we still have a long way to go. But this is an excellent start to what we as a people are capable of doing."

Matthew held his cup high in the air. "Let's toast to the future for our race and for the country. I do sincerely believe that we are on our way to a better country for everyone, and President Obama will begin that journey tomorrow."

"And I thank God that He allowed me to live long enough to witness this great moment in history. I will be right up front in the morning and I'll be thanking God for bringing a beleaguered people to the brink of greatness." I finished my hot chocolate and we returned to the living room where the women were still deep in conversation.

The next day Rubye and I took our seats on the Mall six rows back from the podium where the dignitaries were filing onto and taking their seats. We watched as Vice-President Dick Cheney, looking sick and tired, with his wife took their seats behind where soon to be ex-President George Bush would sit. Then Supreme Court Chief Justice John Roberts climbed the stairs and positioned himself close to where the new president would be sworn in. We burst with pride as we stared at Michelle's mother, with the two little girls, make their way to their place and were seated by what appeared to be the secret service. After another fifteen minutes we smiled again as a tall handsome Black man with a beautiful Black woman next to him entered from the back of the stage accompanied by President George Bush, who displayed his usual smirk, and his wife Barbara.

As I stared up at history being made right in front of me, I couldn't help but recall the classrooms in Union, with old wooden benches in a two story red brick building and a number of young Black men and women sitting and listening to the wise words of a man we called Prof. Sims tell us that he wouldn't live to see this day, but it was possible that we might. I imagined Grandpa Sanders marching right into the middle of a group of angry white men determined to lynch his brother, but he spoiled their plans by grabbing the frightened Black man by his arm and taking him out of trouble. I had a quick vision of Reverend Bates telling me to make sure to always be on time to light that fire under the old steel stove so that the students at Benedict would not miss their breakfast.

As the Chief Justice of the United States Supreme Court stood in front of Obama and stretched out his hand with the Bible in it, I thought of the time in Lukesville where I began my teaching career. I wondered what happened to Billy, the young man in overalls who was curious about education and wanted to some day go to college. Hopefully, he was somewhere watching this great event unfold in front of us. And hopefully, he came to realize that the sacrifices made by his father and millions of other farmers and laborers made it possible for this Black man to take the reigns of power in the most powerful country in the world. This was a collective effort that spanned back to the end of slavery and transcended the dark days of apartheid, and culminated with the victories of a people who brought us all up the rough side of the mountain.

I smiled as Justice Roberts asked Obama to repeat the oath of office. When it was over Obama flashed that million-dollar smile and Michelle followed with a beautiful smile of her own. Justice Roberts took his seat and the 44th President of the United States began to share his feelings with the world.

While he was delivering his acceptance speech, my thoughts were racing so fast it practically made me dizzy. Again I thought of that Minister at Clemson University who told Dean Riley that the future for concerned clergy would involve spending some time in jail. At that moment I felt very proud of my profession, because ministers from all denominations and all colors played a major role in the change that made it possible for me to sit and watch a Black man sworn in as President. I knew that God had to be smiling down, pleased with our accomplishments all done in His name by His servants.

We remembered, we prayed and we celebrated.

< The Spiritual Journey of a Legend >

EPILOGUE

I have been back from Gaffney for a little over a week and was busy writing up my notes on Reverend Sanders' story when my cell phone rang. As I reach for it, I know what this call is all about and I do not want to answer. But it is one of those regretful exercises in life that you cannot run from. The call is from James W. Sanders, Jr., and there is probably only one reason he is calling me.

"Good evening Reverend Sanders," I greet him.

"Toschia, he is gone," is all he says. I can feel the pain and the heartbreak in his voice. "He went home at four o'clock this afternoon," he says.

"How is your mother?" I ask. During the time I was in Gaffney interviewing Reverend Sanders I came to know his wife quite well. She is a wonderful woman who has made many contributions to the progress of our race in her own right. But she was content to be the woman behind the man, as Reverend Sanders grew and prospered as a leader in Gaffney.

"She's holding up fine," James says and then pauses. "I guess as fine as can be expected from someone who just lost a mate who had been with her for 58 years."

"That is a long time and I imagine you can say with certainty and much clarity that they had become one and that is what love is all about."

"No doubt they loved each other. Daddy used to say all the time that she was the woman he loved and he meant it."

221

"I know that's right. One thing I found out in the time I spent with him if Dr. Sanders said something, he definitely meant it."

"We're going to miss him and this city and state are also going to miss him."

I can detect James's sadness and his words are tear filled. I can't find the right words so I just wait for him to continue.

"You know the family wants you here for the celebration of his moving on home to be with God. Every dignitary in the state will be here and I just know Congressman Clyburn will also be here."

"When is the service?" I ask.

"It'll be Tuesday, July 10 at 5:00 p.m."

"I'll make my reservation in the morning."

"Bless you Toschia and you know you have one major responsibility now, don't you?"

I knew he was referring to the story and bringing Dr. Sanders back to life, through the written word. With his autobiography, he would be real and alive for generations to come. That is how he wanted it and he made certain that we were able to finish before he put on his traveling shoes.

"Yes sir, I do," I say with extreme humility.

"When can you get started?"

"I had already began to listen to his tapes and put his words on paper, then I'll sort it all out and get busy writing."

"Good," Sanders says. "In the meantime we'll see you in a couple days so that we can celebrate your friend and my father's homegoing. We know he is already sitting in his mansion and we want to celebrate for him" He finishes and we hang up,

On Tuesday morning I arrive in Gaffney in plenty of time for the service scheduled for five in the afternoon at Bethel. I experience a myriad of feelings as I drive up and park in front of the Sanders's home. There is a line of cars parked in the front and I can tell the activity has already begun inside the house. I think how tough this must be for Mrs. Sanders. She has spent the past fifty-eight years of her life with her husband. That loss has to create a void that will be difficult to fill. She does have her two daughters, her son and a number of grandchildren. And she also has her entire church family, members who have been a part of her life from the time she walked down the aisle at Bethel and married the church's minister.

A slight smile breaks through the sadness all over my face as I think of the time during our interview that Reverend Sanders described the scene when they first arrived back from their honeymoon and attended church that Sunday. Many of the ladies boycotted the church because he had married someone outside the Bethel family. That didn't last long; after all how could they not come back and be part of such a dynamic ministry. Many of the original members are now gone, but their daughters and grand daughters will be there this evening supporting this magnificent woman. That should make her feel real good.

Before I can knock, the door swings open and a young lady invites me inside. I greet her and stroll back to the kitchen where everyone has congregated. I hurry over to Mrs. Sanders, hug her and then I hug Jewette and Ruzlin.

"We are so glad you are here," Mrs. Sanders says.

"How are you feeling?" I ask.

"Warm, content and loved," she says.

"Brother is on his way," Jewette says, speaking of James Jr. "I believe he wants you to sing this evening."

I am somewhat surprised and moved by the family's gesture toward me. I had sung before at the church during service and Reverend Sanders told me I had a voice blessed by God. For the family to now allow me to participate in the service means that I am indeed a part of the family.

"I would be honored," I say.

"We know it's late notice but we have been so busy trying to put two services together, much has been done on short notice," Ruzlin adds.

James Jr. swings open the back door, strolls inside and smiles at me.

"You made it," he says. "We're glad you're here because that means a great deal to Daddy."

He speaks as though Reverend Sanders is still living, but knows that he has moved on. He evidently feels his father's spirit and essence is still there. He is now head of the family and that must be a heavy load for him, following in the footsteps of such a giant. James Jr. came to the ministry much later than his father but no doubt would become an excellent leader for Bethel; he was taught by the best.

"I can think of no other place I could possibly be except here with the family," I say.

"I understand you finished the interviews and now are beginning to work on the story," he says.

"Yes, in fact I have already started to listen to the tapes. There are a number of other people I want to interview, including the family. But that can wait until you all get through the business you have to take care of."

"It's important that we do this, because it is something he definitely wanted done," James says. "God allowed him to stay here until he finished giving you his life story, and that tells us all this is something God also wants done."

"How was last night's service at Island Creek?" I ask.

"Outstanding," James replies. "Probably as not a big of a crowd that we'll have today at Bethel, but some very distinguished and important people were there. And of course the Omegas did their Order of the Omegas and Congressman Clyburn spoke."

"How was the Congressman?"

"Also outstanding. His remarks resonated with everyone in the audience. You know he's also an Omega and that made his remarks all the more personal. He said Daddy would become a legend in the annals of South Carolina history, and will someday be recognized by the entire country for his achievements." James pauses to let his words resonate with me. He did it for a reason. "And you and your company will make that happen when you write his life story for the entire world to read. That's why we must get busy and get it written as soon as possible."

"I agree and I have people working with me so that we will make it happen."

"Are you hungry, young lady?" Mrs. Sanders ask. "Jewette, lets get this girl fed," she continues before I can answer.

Jewette signals for me to follow her. We go into the dining area where the table is overflowing with food. "Folks been bringing food all day long. You got everything you can imagine. You got breakfast food, lunch, dinner and late night snack food," she says with a chuckle.

"You have to sing "His Eyes are on the Sparrow," she says as I get a plate and begin to load it up with bacon, breakfast potatoes, eggs and toast. "He just loved the way you sang that song at church just a…," she cannot finish as her voice is choked and her eyes fill with tears. "He's really gone and this place will not be the same ever again," she says.

"I know," I agree. "It'll never be the same whenever I come back here."

"And we want you to come back as often as possible. You know you're family, and we want you to ride in one of the family limousines this afternoon," she says.

I find a seat at the table and begin to eat. "I need to eat and get over to the hotel and check in," I say. "I came here straight from the airport."

"Take your time, enjoy your breakfast," Jewette says just like a big sister. "Service isn't until five o'clock. You just need to be back here about four."

"Thank you," I say and gulp down another fork full of eggs.

Jewette turns and walks back into the kitchen to be with her mother. I sit there consuming my breakfast, still not convinced that I am there for Reverend Sanders' funeral, because I am still not convinced he is gone. I am sure that I won't feel the finality of the act until I walk into Bethel that evening and acknowledge that this entire event is happening because he is really gone. I know that his spirit will be with us and that is so re-assuring of his greatness.

My first impression when I walk into the church and stare at Reverend Sanders lying peaceful and still in the casket, is that he remains a very handsome and distinguished looking man, even in death. I decided not to ride with the family. I called Jewette and told her I would meet them at the church. She insists that I sit in the front row to the right of where the family will be. I get there before the family arrives, and the usher expects me. He escorts me to the front row and I will be to the right of Mrs. Sanders. It is only four-thirty and the church is packed.

I sit and listen as a minister reads passages from the Old and New Testament. It is difficult for me to keep my eyes from wandering over to the casket where Reverend Sanders lies peacefully, oblivious to all that is happening around him. I know, as does everyone else in the church, that he is gone and it reminds me of the passage from the Bible that says, "Absent from the body, present with the Lord." It is difficult to comprehend such a transition. Just a week ago I was visiting him in the hospital and now he has met and talked with Jesus. That is a transition almost impossible for the human mind to understand. But it is through faith that we accept that transition from this life to the next.

Finally the dignitaries begin the march down the center aisle and take their seats right behind where the family will sit. A smile crosses my face because I probably know more about this wonderful man than most people in the church. For over a week I traveled with him through his life. I feel privileged to know that he trusted and believed in me to the point that he shared his entire life with me, and now I will have the opportunity to share it with the rest of the world through the written word. Everyone stands as the family makes their way down the aisle and to their pew in the first four rows. Mrs. Sanders has her arm inside James Jr.'s arm, as he escorts his mother. She looks dignified, strong and stoic in appearance. Jewette, Ruzlin, Marionette, and the members of the family follow behind. They stroll to their seats. Some look down at Reverend Sanders and others choose not to.

Once the procession is over, the Bethel Baptist Church Combined Choir stands to their feet and fills the room with melodious sounds.

"*When the shadows of this life have gone,*

I'll fly away.

Like a bird from prison bars has flown,

226

The Life of Reverend James W. Sanders

I'll fly away, Oh Glory, I'll fly away

When I die, Hallelujah, by and by

I'll fly away."

The service is beautiful in all ways. Speakers from all the different organizations Reverend Sanders belonged to bring words of adoration for him and consolation for the family. Congressman John Spratt, one of Reverend Sander's closest allies in the many battles to integrate South Carolina, reads a special statement from President Barack Obama. Steve Pelissier, Executive Director of the Appalachian Council of Government, reads a letter from Ex-President Bill Clinton. Reverend C.V. Owens speaks briefly about his long friendship with Reverend Sanders and how much the man had meant to him. Many of the deacons from the church praise him for his leadership.

Finally it is my turn to sing. There is only one song he would want me to sing for him. I try to keep my composure and not cry. This man is like a grandfather to me and I feel the loss deep in my soul. But I will make it through for him.

As I begin, I just pray that my legs don't give out before I finish.

"Why should I feel discouraged,

Why should the shadows come,

Why should my heart feel lonely away from my heavenly home

When Jesus is my potion

My constant friend is He

For His eye is on the sparrow

And I know He watches me

So I sing because I'm happy

I sing because I'm free

His eye is on the sparrow

And I know he watches me."

I feel good inside. I know that God is watching over all of us as we say our final goodbye to someone we all love. I finish and make my way back to my seat. I sing because I am happy and I am happy at that moment.

For the next hour, more dignitaries make their way up to the podium and praise Reverend Sanders. It has been nearly three hours since the service began and his admirers continue to make their way to the front and tell the over fourteen hundred mourners what he meant to them in their lives. I regain my composure when they lower the lights and begin a video review of Reverend Sanders. Pictures of him as a child, as a young man, as a college student and then as the minister of Bethel flash by us giving everyone a glimpse of over eighty years of personal history. The picture that gets to me more than any of the others is the one of him and Mrs. Sanders on their wedding day. They were an absolutely beautiful couple. No wonder he always referred to her as the most beautiful woman to ever be in his life.

Once the video ends, we all watch as his grandchildren and his sister Marionette come to the pulpit and pay homage to his memory. And then finally, the one man closest to Reverend Sanders in his life, Reverend Malachi Duncan strolls to the pulpit with his Bible in hand and his glasses down on his nose. He pauses to catch his breath. After a brief few seconds he speaks.

"This is a man I have known since he was a child growing up in the small country town of Union, South Carolina," he says. "When he was just a little boy I used to take him by the hand and lead him to school. Then when the war came I went off to help fight for this country and did not see him again until I returned to go to Benedict College. By that time, he was an ordained preacher. Can you believe that he was a preacher by seventeen, and for the next sixty-five years held on to God's unchanging hand. He preached the Gospel as it was constantly revealed to him through the Holy Spirit." Malachi pauses and looks down at the casket. "Rest in the arms of the Lord, my friend," he says. "Long time ago, we both promised that whoever lived longest would preach the other one's homegoing service." This great man pauses again as I can tell he has become slightly choked up.

I want to rush up there and help him because I know, as does everyone else sitting and listening, that this is very difficult for him. But he manages and continues.

228

The Life of Reverend James W. Sanders

"I'm nine years older than Reverend Sanders so I always thought it would be him preaching over me, and I always felt good knowing that such an outstanding preacher would help send me off to Heaven. With his prayers and his final words over me, there is no way the gates of Heaven wouldn't open up for me. I just pray that my words are sufficient to the Lord so that I do my part to send my friend out of this world in a way fitting for a man of his stature."

For the next ten minutes, Reverend Malachi Duncan touches the entire congregation with his words. But the most emotional moment comes when he begins to sing Reverend Sander's trademark song, "Traveling Shoes." He is so effective within minutes he has the entire congregation joining in with him. During those final few minutes of a very special time in the history of Gaffney, South Carolina and Bethel Baptist Church, joy abounds. Men and women who came to say goodbye to the man they love actually end up saying good morning to the dawning of a new day for Reverend Sanders. It is a new day because as the song says "I'll Fly Away," that is what he did, he flew away to be with his Savior, and for the eighty-one years he was here, Reverend James W. Sanders Sr., helped to make this a better place for all of the people here in Gaffney and throughout the state of South Carolina.

A POEM OF REMEMBRANCE

Make room for you to bloom

Why not?

Here we are, so near each other, yet

Each of us with our very own spot

We grow, we blossom at our own pace

Your blossoming out,

Gently touches and steadily moves me aside

Remember, it was you

Permitting me to lean on you

That was the strength beneath my last blossom

Not you?

Does it really matter my friend?

I am here strong at the moment.

Lean on me.

Grow and blossom

Your beauty enhances me until

I can bloom again

Marionette Sanders-Daniels

www.ingramcontent.com/pod-product-compliance
Lightning Source LLC
Chambersburg PA
CBHW021050090426
42738CB00006B/265